With the Flying Squadron

FLIGHT–LIEUT. HAROLD ROSHER, R.N.

With the Flying Squadron

Letters of a Pilot of the
Royal Naval Air Service
During the First World War

Harold Rosher

LEONAUR

With the Flying Squadron
Letters of a Pilot of the
Royal Naval Air Service
During the First World War
by Harold Rosher

First published under the title
With the Flying Squadron

Leonaur is an imprint
of Oakpast Ltd

ISBN: 978-0-85706-304-5 (hardcover)
ISBN: 978-0-85706-303-8 (softcover)

http://www.leonaur.com

Contents

Introduction

BY ARNOLD BENNETT

Harold Rosher was born at Beckenham on the 18th November, 1893, and was educated at The Dene, Caterham, and subsequently at Woodbridge. Although as a boy he suffered severely from acute asthma and bronchitis, he did well at school; and the pluck which carried him through the moral distresses of asthma helped him to hold his own in games, despite the fact that up to the age of sixteen he was considerably under the average height. As his health did not cease to give anxiety, he was taken for a holiday to India (being with his father the guest of the Maharajah Ranjitsinhji, Jam Sahib of Nawanagar) in 1909. In 1913, for the same reason, he made a trip to South Africa with his sister. It was his health again which helped to decide his career. An open-air life was considered to be essential, and he became a student at the South Eastern Agricultural College, Wye, remaining there until the outbreak of the war.

One of Harold's greatest chums at the Agriculture College was a young and rich German landowner named K——. At the latter's invitation Harold spent the summer vacation of 1913 in Germany, and the two young men toured on motor-cycles through a great part of Germany and Austria. In August 1914 K—— was to celebrate his majority, and had asked Harold to the festivities. But on August 2nd, when war appeared inevitable, he wrote a letter of farewell to Harold in which he said that he did not expect they would ever meet again. The next day he telephoned from Charing Cross as he was leaving England, and Harold was overheard saying to him on the telephone: "Well, if we meet, mind you don't shoot straight."

On the day of the declaration of war, Harold applied for a commission in the Royal Naval Air Service, and in order to save time he went immediately as a civilian pupil to Brooklands, where several months previously he had once been taken up in the air as a passenger. In the few days which elapsed before the War Office commandeered the Brooklands Aerodrome and ejected every civilian Harold progressed rapidly in the craft of flying. He was gazetted a probationary flight sub-lieutenant in the R.N.A.S. on August 18th and reported himself at Hendon. He remained there about six weeks, obtaining his aviator's certificate.

The letters which form this book were written between August 1914 and February 1916, They are spontaneous and utterly unstudied documents, and they have been printed almost exactly as Harold wrote them. Many of them are quite ordinary; most are spiced with slang; the long ones describing his share in the great historic raids are thrillingly dramatic. But it would not be wise to set some letters above others. None should be missed. Each contributes its due realistic share to the complete picture of an airman's life in war.

It is well that we should have every opportunity of estimating what that life is. For the air service is still quite a new service. Its birth lies within the memory of schoolboys. Few outsiders can imaginatively conceive for themselves the conditions of it, conditions in which the hour of greatest danger is precisely the hour of spiritual solitude and separation from all mankind. Further, the air service is now actually engaged in creating those superb precedents which members of the older services find ready for their fortifying and encouragement when the crisis comes, and this fact alone entitles it to a most special sympathetic attention from the laity. So far as my knowledge goes, no other such picture, so full and so convincing, of the air-fighters' existence has yet been offered to the public Here, perhaps, I may mention that some organs of the London Press long ago desired to print the principal descriptive letters of Harold Rosher, which in private had aroused the admiration of journalists and literary men; but it was felt that complete publication of the entire series within the covers of a volume would be more proper and more effective.

Three days after the date of the last letter Harold was killed. On 27th February, Major Risk, the C.O. of the Dover Aeroplane Station being away on duty, Harold, as second in command, was in charge. Among other duties he had to train new pilots on fast machines, and he would always personally test a new machine or a newly-repaired machine before allowing anybody else to try it. On that Sunday morning he ordered a number of machines to be brought out of the sheds for practice flights. Among them was one which had just been repaired after a mishap three weeks earlier. The pilot had already got into his machine. Harold told him to get out as the machine was untested, and himself took it up for a trial flight of eight or ten minutes.

Everything seemed to go right until Harold began the descent about a mile away from the aerodrome. Then, at a height of 300 feet or less, the machine suddenly made a nosedive and crashed to the ground. Harold was killed instantly. The disaster occupied seven seconds. At the inquest nothing was ascertained as to the cause of the accident. One theory is that the controls jammed. Harold was buried on the 2nd of March at Charlton Cemetery, with full naval honours. The cemetery is on the cliffs within sight of the aerodrome, and while his body was being lowered into the grave aeroplanes were flying overhead. It is permissible to quote a few Service opinions about Harold Rosher's attainments and achievements during his short career as an airman. Commodore Murray F. Sueter, C.B., R. N., wrote to Mr. Frank Rosher, Harold's father:

> In my opinion he was one of our best pilots; always ready for any service he was called upon to perform. Mr. Winston Churchill was very pleased with his work in the early part of the war, and had he been spared I am sure he would have made a great name for himself." Wing Commander Arthur N. Longmore, R.N., under whom Harold had served longest, wrote:
> You have the consolation of knowing his splendid record at Dunkirk. He was among the finest pilots I ever had out there, always cheerful and ready for his work. He will be a great loss to the Air Service, which loses not only a first-class pilot, but also an excellent officer." Major Charles E. Risk, Squadron Commander, R. N., wrote: "Harold, or Rosh as we always used to call him, was one of my very best pals and a very fine officer and First Lieutenant Everyone loved him. He was an absolute 'Sahib,' a very good pilot, hard-working, and absolutely trustworthy.

And Captain Charles L. Lamb, R.N., wrote:

> He returned with some of the others from abroad last autumn for a rest, and very shortly afterwards I selected him from a large number of officers to become the Executive Officer of the Dover Air Station, which was then starting. Although quite young, he immediately displayed great organising abilities, and also possessed the gift of command of men, which is unusual

without previous training, and fully justified my selection. At his own request he was shortly proceeding abroad in command of a Flight, and would undoubtedly have gained his promotion in the near future. I have said little as regards his skill as a pilot, since this was probably well known to you, but he was undoubtedly in the first flight. This skill, however, I consider of secondary importance in life as compared with the far rarer gifts of command and organisation which he undoubtedly possessed.

I had the acquaintance of Harold Kosher, and when I met him I was quite extraordinarily impressed by his bearing and his speech. In age and appearance he was a mere boy—a handsome boy, too, in my opinion—but the gestures of youth were restrained. He was very modest, but he was not diffident. In the presence of men older than his father he upheld in the most charming and effective way the dignity of his own generation. He talked quietly, but nobody could escape the conviction that he knew just what he was talking about. All his statements were cautious, and in giving a description or an opinion he seemed to dread superlatives. He had the eye and the voice of one who feared no responsibility, and who, having ruled himself, was thoroughly equal to ruling others. He was twenty-two when he died at work.

A.B.

FLIGHT-LIEUT. RIGGALL
IN ONE OF THE GRAHAME-WHITE SCHOOL "BOX-KITES," IN THE EARLY
DAYS OF HIS TRAINING.

1

Training

1

To his Father

The Blue Bird, Brooklands Aerodrome,
Weybridge.
11th August, 1914.

Dear Dad,

Am getting on famously and having a most amusing time. After I wrote you yesterday I went out and had my first lesson. Mr. Stutt, our instructor [for the British and Colonial Aeroplane C.O.], sits immediately behind you, controls the engine switch and covers your hand on the stick. He took me straight up two or three hundred feet and then volplaned down. He always does this with new pupils to see how they take it. I think I managed to pass the ordeal all right. I had two or three flights backwards and forwards, and then another turn later on in the evening. Stutt is an awfully nice fellow, very small but very capable.

On all sides one hears him recommended. When in the air, he bawls in your ear, "Now when you push your hand forward, you go down, see!" (and he pushes your hand forward and you make a sudden dive), "and when you pull it back you go up, and when you do this, so and so happens," and so with everything he demonstrates. Then he says, "If you do so and so, you will break your neck, and if you try to climb too quickly you will make a tail slide." It's awfully hard work at first and makes your arm ache like fun. The school machines are very similar to the Grahame-Whites. You sit right in front, with a clean drop below you. We never strap ourselves in. The machines are the safest known, and never make a clean drop if control is lost, but slide down sideways.

When it got too dark we went in and had dinner, all sitting at the middle table. Could get no one to fetch my luggage, so decided to go myself after dinner. Unfortunately, I attempted a short cut in the dark and lost my way. After stumbling round the beastly aerodrome in the dark for an hour, I eventually got back to my starting point. I was drenched to the knees, and the moon didn't help me much on account of the thick mist. It was about 10.30 p. m., so I gave up my quest; the prospect of the long walk and heavy bag was too discouraging.

I turned in in my vest and pants and had a good night. Was knocked up at 4.30 this morning and crawled gingerly into my still wet clothes. A lovely morning, very cold, and it was not long before I got wetter still, as the grass was sopping. Had two more lessons this morning, of about 15 minutes each, and took both right and left hand turns, part of the time steering by myself. Stutt says I am getting on. The machines are so stable that they will often fly quite a long way by themselves. Am now quite smitten, and if weather continues fine, I shall take my ticket in a week or ten days. Hope to be flying solo by Thursday or Friday. Experienced my first bump this morning. While flying at 200 feet, the machine suddenly bumped,[1] a unique sensation. These bumps are due to the sun's action on the air and are called "sun bumps." It's owing to these that we novices are not allowed to fly during the day. To experienced airmen they offer no difficulty.

There was a slight accident here this morning. One of the Blériot people (known in our select circle as Blérites) was taxying [running along the ground] in a machine without wings. He got too much speed on, and the machine went head over heels and was utterly wrecked—man unhurt. With the Blériot machine you first have to learn to steer on the ground, as it's much harder than ours. The men look awful fools going round and round in wee circles. . . .

Very nice lot of fellow pupils here that I am getting to know, one naval man with a whole stock of funny yarns. Nothing to do all day long but sleep. Went into Weybridge this morning and got my suit case. *Flora* and *fauna* quite interesting. I live only for the mornings and evenings. More *anon*. Love to all.

Ever your loving son,
Harold.

---

1. Met an air-wave.

2

TO HIS FATHER

The Hendon Aerodrome, Hendon.
7th September, 1914.

Dear Dad,

Only a few lines, as it is already late, and I still have plenty to do. The latest excitement down here is a balloon, especially for our use. It is to be up all night, and we have to take turns in keeping watch from it; four hour shifts, starting tomorrow night. She has 4,000 feet of wire cable, but I don't suppose we shall be up more than 1,500 feet. It will be frightfully cold work, and in all probability we shall all be seasick.

On Saturday night we had a Zeppelin scare from the Admiralty. I was on duty and called out the marines, etc., etc. Ammunition was served round and the machines brought out. Porte [J. C. Porte, Wing Commander, R.N.] went up for a short time.

Tons of love.

Ever your loving son,
Harold.

3

TO HIS GRANDMOTHER

The Hendon Aerodrome, Hendon.
7th September, 2914.

Dearest Granny,

Can only send you a few lines just now as I am so frightfully busy. Thanks so much for your letter received two days back Am hard at it now from 4.30 a.m. to 11.0 p.m., and one day in five for 24 hours on end. Our latest acquaintance is a captive balloon in which we are to take turns to keep watch in the night. It will be terribly cold work. The watches are 4 hours each, and we shall probably be about 1,500 feet up in the air—the full limit of cable is 4,000 feet. I quite expect we shall all be horribly seasick, as the motion is quite different from that in an aeroplane. There is also a rumour that we are going to have an airship down here. We had a Zeppelin scare the other night and had all the marines out, ammunition served round, searchlights manned, and aeroplanes brought out in readiness. It was quite exciting for a false alarm.

It's pretty chilly work sleeping in tents now. Unless you cover your clothes up overnight, they are sopping wet in the morning. Also there is a plague of crane flies here, which simply swarm all over one's tent.

15

These are all little troubles, however, which one takes philosophically, and at the same time tries to picture mentally the distress of those at the front. Hope I shall be out there soon; they seem to be having quite good fun.

Must cut short now, so goodbye, Granny dear. Heaps of love.

Ever your loving grandson,

Harold.

4

To his Father

The Hendon Aerodrome, Hendon.

11th September, 1914

Dear Dad,

Many happy returns. I started writing you last night, so that you might get my letter first thing this morning, but was fated not to finish it. We had another false alarm and my place was on the 'phones. I didn't get off until 12.30 a.m., so gave it up as a bad job and started afresh this morning.

I expect you will have seen in the papers about the accident last night. Lieut. G—— went up in the Henri Farman, and on coming down made a bad landing—internal injuries—machine absolutely piled up. Nacelle[2] telescoped and the tail somehow right in front of the nacelle. The accident is expected to have rather a bad effect on the *morale* of the pupils. Personally it doesn't affect me; and anyhow I didn't see G—— at all, as I was bound to the 'phones.

Things are going on much better with me. Yesterday I did five straights [straight flights] alone and managed quite well, having excellent control of the machine, and making good landings, except for the first straights in the morning, when it was rather windy and in consequence the machine was all over the place.

By the way, this is now the third successive night that we have had an alarm. Have not yet been up in the balloon but am looking forward to it. I never thought that we should come down to an old (1902) gas bag.

Heaps of love and don't let Mummie get alarmed. You must bear in mind that night flying is ten times more dangerous than day.

Ever your loving son,

Harold.

---

2. The nacelle is the short body of an aeroplane, as found in all machines with propeller behind (usually called "pusher" machines).

Note

An interesting letter, written in September, is missing. In this the writer described a balloon trip that he made over London in the dark, ultimately coming down near Ashford, and having an exciting experience while landing.

Early in October, 1914, the aviator went from Hendon to the Royal Naval Air Station, Fort Grange, Gosport. A letter of this date is also missing. It described his first cross-country flight, when, owing to engine failure, he had to make three forced landings (from heights of about 4,000 feet), all of which he managed safely without damaging his machine. The engine was afterwards found to be faulty. In this letter he referred to the commanding officer's pleasure that he had made so good a beginning.

2

On Home Service

5

To his Father

Royal Naval Air Station,
Fort Grange, Gosport
14th November, 1914.

Dear Dad,

Many thanks for note received this morning. Shall try to get home for inoculation in about a fortnight. From what I can make out, we shall not get our squadron together until the end of January. We were to have gone over at the end of this month. We may, however, go over in pieces, a flight at a time. If the Germans reach Calais, we shall stay here permanently for home defence, but at the rate we are progressing, we shan't be ready until March, and then, maybe, the war will be over. I must say I want to see some of it, and one would be bound to get a second stripe if one went across.

15th November, 1914.

Have spent quite a successful first day over at Whale Island:—squad drill, Morriss tube and Webley Scott firing practice. I got on famously. The Morriss tube is particularly easy. It merely becomes a matter of getting all on the bull. It's a grand place to wake one up; everything is done at the double.

My cold is awfully heavy and I'm feeling pretty rotten.

Best love.

Ever your loving son,
Harold.

6

The Queen's Hotel, Farnborough, Hants.
18th November, 1914.

Dear Dad,

Thanks so much for your birthday letter [his 21st birthday], which I had just time hurriedly to read through this morning. Late last night we had orders to shift, and everything has been a rush ever since. I have left all my luggage at Fort Grange and have only a small despatch case with me. Am very disappointed. As the C.O.'s machine was not ready to go, he collared mine, and I am travelling as passenger. However, it can't be helped.

We left Fort Grange about ten this morning and arrived here after an hour's run. It was awfully cold and we had to come down here owing to fog. I am afraid I can't tell you where we are going or any other such details. You must rest content with what I have told you at present. We are very comfortably fixed up here for the night. The place is packed with generals and staff officers, as we are practically in Aldershot. It will be very slow here this evening. I thought of trying to get home for the night, but it's out of the question. There is no need to be in the least alarmed as to my safety, as I am probably not going where you expect.

Tons of love.

Ever your loving son,
Harold.

7

To his Father

Royal Naval Air Station, Kenton Lodge,
Gosforth, Newcastle-on-Tyne.
25th November, 1914.

Dear Dad,

Received letters forwarded from Fort Grange last night. It was much too foggy for my trip to Hartlepool yesterday afternoon, but I went for a short flip [flight] around, and am glad I did so, as I found out the lie of the land.

This morning it was beautifully clear, and I started off soon after 9.0 a. m., with a mechanic, to patrol the coast up north to Alnmouth. It was awfully cold with rather a strong cross wind. I got right above one lot of clouds. It's a wonderful sight too, as in the distance there is a mountain covered with snow. It was simply ripping. My engine was going strong, and after circling round till I was 1,500 feet up, I made straight off for the coast. It was magnificent. Anything I wanted to look at closely I just did graceful spirals around, or zigzagged, banking the machine up to right and left. I have never enjoyed a trip so much before. I was away an hour and twenty minutes; quite long enough, as I could hardly feel my hands or feet on coming down. I think we shall be here another fortnight, with luck.

30th November, 1914.

Have had no time to write at all these last few days. Half my birthday letters are still unanswered. . . . Weather has been far too bad for flying the past two days.

Best love to all.

Ever your loving son,
Harold.

8

TO HIS AUNT

Royal Naval Air Station, Kenton Lodge,
Gosforth, Newcastle-on-Tyne.
27th November, 1914.

Dear Aunt Ethel,

Thanks so much for your birthday letter. I only received it the night before last and have been unable to answer it until now.

You are right about flying. As soon as one gets well into the air, things seem to take on quite a different aspect. It is the same as when one gets on a high hill, only in a greater degree. Our work of patrolling the coast is very interesting, but unfortunately Newcastle seems to be either enveloped in a thick fog, or a gale of wind prevails, so that we are not getting as much flying as I should like. It is beginning to get extremely cold work too now, especially on a frosty morning.

Our billet here happens to be the German Consulate, a lovely modern house, so that we are most comfortably settled. I think we are moving again in a fortnight's time. Please give Granny my best love. As soon as I can get home I shall pop over and look you all up. At present I see no chance of getting off. I tried to get to Hartlepool this morning, but the weather was too bad so I abandoned the attempt.

Heaps of love.

Ever your loving nephew,
Harold.

9

To his Father

No. 1 Naval Aeroplane Squadron,
Kenton Lodge, Newcastle-on-Tyne.
8th December, 1914.

Dear Dad,

Have had a great day. Motored out to Redcar on business and visited Durham Cathedral on the return journey. It's a magnificent spot. The Cathedral is on top of a high hill with the river flowing through a ravine on one side and two fine old bridges. It's one of the finest sights in England. The town itself, too, is very quaint. Have heard no more about going to the front...

10th December, 1914.[1]

The C.O. is now in France, and from what I can gather is making preparations for us all to go out immediately after Christmas. I don't think there is much chance of being able to get home for Christmas. However, one can never tell, so we will hope for the best.

I went for a flip around yesterday afternoon for ten minutes, but it was far too thick to see anything, so came down. Best love.

Ever your loving son,
Harold.

10

To his Mother

Hotel Burlington, Dover.
30th December, 1914.

Dearest Mum,

Another sudden move. Monday night some of us received orders to shift here the following morning. I got all my gear packed and off in the transport first thing, and kept my little handbag in the machine. Two went off before me, as I burst a tyre to begin with—rather a bad start. In my second attempt I got well off, but found my air-speed indicator was not working and my compass dud, so came down again. As I could procure no more, I decided to start. I nearly upset getting off, as my foot slipped on the rudder and I got a bump at the same moment. The engine was going none too well, but I pushed off towards the coast, and all went well for a time.

Then came signs of engine trouble. The revs, [revolutions] dropped

---

1. About this time Lieut. Rosher returned to Fort Grange.

suddenly to below 1,000, and she missed badly and back fired. I at once shut off petrol and volplaned down from 4,000 feet. I glided two miles before I could find a field to satisfy me, but having picked it, made a good landing. Some farmhands and two special constables soon turned up and informed me that I was miles from anywhere. My exact position was between two small villages, Ripe and Chalvington, and four fields away from a road (and that not a main one). The nearest town of any size was Lewes, a matter of seven miles—no motor vehicles, but I might possibly get a trap.

Just then a fellow turned up, and said he had a motor bike and side car, which he put at my disposal. This I accepted, and, after trying the engine, left the two special constables in charge, and tramped across the four swamped fields (up to my neck in mud) to the road, and went to Lewes in the side car. There I found a big garage, where they professed to know something about Gnome engines. (I had landed, by the way, at about 12 noon.) I got them to put some tools on a car, and out we went again to Ripe. Then followed much tinkering, and I got the engine going and started off. I had circled round once, when the engine again back fired, bang! Bang! and I made another hurried descent two fields away from the last. All this time, of course, quite a crowd had collected, and the vicar of Chalvington had come up and had brought me some sandwiches, for which I was very grateful, it being 3.0 p. m., and I had only a hurried breakfast.

We next ran the engine again, and she at once backfired and caught fire at the carburettor. This burnt out without doing any damage, and we diagnosed the complaint as a broken inlet valve-spring in No. 5 cylinder. By the way, when in Lewes I had 'phoned through to Fort Grange, and they sent me on some mechanics, as the garage men could help me no more.

I once more left the special constables in charge and returned to Lewes. (The vicar, I should have told you, offered me a bed for the night.) I again 'phoned from Lewes [to Fort Grange] and then returned to the machine, which I had moved behind a hedge out of the wind, and had pegged and roped down and covered up.

By this time it was 5.30 and dark and very cold, and I was greatly cheered by five mechanics and a driver turning up. Two I left in charge of the machine, and then drove round in our service car (in which the mechanics had arrived) to the vicarage, where I had a belated tea and a hearty welcome. Mrs. McElroy is delightful. Dinner followed almost immediately, and very excellent at that. At 8.0 p.m. my car arrived

Bringing the pilot ashore after a flight on a Sopwith seaplane

"Short" seaplanes at anchor off Spithead

for me, the mechanics having found a satisfactory billet. I once more set out for Lewes and rattled out the colonel of the territorials, and requested a corporal and three men to guard my machine, as my men had been working the whole of the previous night.

This all took some time, so I sat down and chatted with the other members of the staff, and had a drink and smoke, and also two trunk calls, one to Dover and the other to Fort Grange, where I heard that Riggall [2] had also come down with engine trouble at Hastings, 30 miles further on. This cheered me considerably. I didn't get away from Lewes till 1 0.0 p. m. At Ripe I posted my territorials and gave them their orders. It was fortunately a lovely moonlight night, freezing hard, and with no wind. I got back to the vicarage at 11.30 p. m. and retired at midnight—a lovely hot bath and beautifully soft bed, with a fire in my room!

I turned out next morning at daylight and drove out to the machine, which is an 80 Avro,[3] brand new (never been flown before, not even been tested), and found my men at work as per instructions. I returned for breakfast (the vicarage was a good two miles away) , and then rushed back to my machine and found that a C.P.O. [Chief Petty Officer] had turned up from Gosport in another car, on his way to Riggall at Hastings, with a whole new engine. I at once hot-stuffed [requisitioned] one of his inlet valves and set the men to work changing it, while I once more went into Lewes, looked up the colonel and used his 'phone.

On getting back at 12.30 I found my machine all ready, so went on to the vicarage, packed up my things, had a slice of cake, bade them all farewell, and pushed off. The wind had got up considerably and the clouds were very low, but I thought I would try and get off. I started up and got well away. It was awfully bumpy, and I got tossed about all over the place. When I got to 1,000 feet it was much steadier, so I headed straight for the coast, and as I climbed, I started getting into the clouds. The first were at 1,500 feet, and I kept on running through them till over 2,500 feet. The wind was stronger than I had thought, and I fairly raced along. The engine was still a bit funny, but I stuck to it, and was past Dungeness in no time.

Then I got right above a whole sea of clouds, and only got occa-

2. Gordon Riggall. He and the writer both received their commissions on the 18th August, 1914, and from that day onwards served together, sharing the same risks. He was killed on the 16th February, 1915.
3. Manufactured by A.V. Roe & C0., Ltd.

sional glimpses of Mother Earth now and again between gaps. I didn't like this, as I couldn't see where I was going, especially as my compass was not accurate, and if I started flying below them, I should only be a thousand feet up. This would have been worse, as I was not sure of my engine, and if it had given out I should have had to land within a mile in any direction, as against a four-mile radius if I were 4,000 feet up.

While thinking over all this, I passed another gap, and looking back, caught a glimpse of Dover harbour. It was rather lucky, as I had overshot the mark. I switched on and off, and dived down through the opening to 1,000 feet, and then looked around for the aerodrome. I did quite a wide circle before I spotted it. It was awfully bumpy and pretty nearly a gale blowing. I was just going to land when I saw two red flags ahead to mark bad ground, and then a lot more. Nearly all the ground was bad, so I flew right over into the wind and turned to the right just before the cliff out of the wind.

All this time I was bobbing about like a cork, gusts throwing me all over the place. I got half round my turn, broadside into the wind at about 100 feet, when a huge gust got underneath my left wing and tail and swept me right across the aerodrome to the ground. It was all a matter of seconds till I hit the ground. My aileron, or warp control, was useless (at the time I thought the wires had broken). I just managed to flatten out and straighten up a little as I hit the ground sideways. Both wheels buckled right up and brought me to a standstill, myself quite unharmed, and the machine with wonderfully little damage. I was awfully annoyed, as I was very keen on pitching well at the end of my journey.

1st January, 1915.

The last two days have been beastly, nothing but wind and rain. Riggall is still held up at Hastings. I shouldn't be surprised if his machine has blown away by now. I see in this morning's paper that I have shipped another stripe [Flight Lieutenant], so things are looking up a bit.

There was a huge din here to usher in the New Year—bells, whistles, and all the ships in the harbour blowing their sirens for fully a quarter of an hour on end. The feeding here is excellent, . and we have music to accompany tea and dinner. There are between three and four hundred rooms, and all full up. We have to take turns in sleeping up at the sheds two miles away (my turn tonight, ugh!). We leave here at 7.45 p. m., and are relieved at 9.0 the next morning. This means 10 o'clock breakfast by the time one has got back here and had a bath and a shave.

What a life we lead and how we suffer! It is now half past six and I have just had tea. My previous meal was a scrappy breakfast at 8.30. Dover is the very devil of a place to fly over. It's very hilly, and so of course one gets the most appalling bumps and, in addition, a very poor selection of landing grounds in case of engine trouble. The aerodrome is right on top of the cliffs, and on two sides we have a beastly drop. If one's engine fails when getting off in these directions, the best thing one can do is to pray, and hope the bump won't be too big when it comes.

I was nearly caught this way today. Yesterday I flew an Avro to Deal and back, while my passenger made some wireless experiments. Today I patrolled the South Foreland for an hour and a half (9.0 to 10.30) , my passenger armed to the teeth. Beastly cold it was too. At one o'clock I got a panicky message saying 14 hostile aircraft were coming over from Dunkirk, and I was ordered up at once. I had just got nicely over the valley when my engine went bang! Bang! Bang! I hastily turned off my petrol and looked around for a place to pitch. The only field reachable was a very bad one. In addition, I pitched badly, but broke nothing, and luckily came to a standstill a few yards from a pond!

The trouble was an inlet valve gone, the same as happened at Lewes, resulting in back firing into the carburettor, which catches fire—most unpleasant. I get awfully cold feet. I would much sooner come down with a bump than be cremated. Personally I think it's worse than the crank shaft breaking, and that puts the fear of God into you, I can tell you. My machine is out in the open tonight. I hope to see it up and get back tomorrow. I did a fine spiral [spiral descent with the engine shut off] today.

The hostile aircraft never came, of course. We are always hearing of Zeppelins dropping bombs on Birmingham, London, etc. All the same, they are coming, I am sure, and in a bunch too.

It's just dinner-time and I'm awfully hungry, so love to all. Could see France as plain as Punch today. Dunkirk is visible from 5,000 feet.

Another day of toil, but no flying. It's my turn to sleep up at the sheds too, a joy I am not looking forward to.

I wish we could get out to the front. It's rotten to keep on seeing army machines going across. I would much rather come to a sticky end out there than here.

23rd January, 1915.

I am once again installed in the sheds for the night, and beastly cold it is too. I am going to invest in a Jaeger flea bag [sleeping bag].

Today has been the best day we have had so far, clear, frosty and dead calm. I crashed into the atmosphere first thing this morning and flipped around for 55 minutes. By then I was as cold as ——, so pitched in the 'drome. I flew from Dover to Deal with both hands off the controls, just correcting with a finger when necessary. I have elastic bands on the stick which hold it where it is set. I ended up with a hair-splitting spiral, with the machine banked up to about 55°. I only did three or four complete turns, but kept on until I was scared stiff. When you bank a machine over 45°, your rudder turns into your elevator and *vice versa*. To come out of a spiral, you just shove everything the wrong way round and wait and see what happens.

Love to all.

Ever your loving son,
Harold.

11

To his Father

Hotel Burlington, Dover.
20th January, 1915.

Dear Dad,

So you are home again at last. Did you get the letters I wrote to Liverpool when you were going off?

There has been very little doing here lately. Awful bobbery last night over the Yarmouth scare. We were standing by our machines until midnight. I think they [the Germans] are sure to pay us a visit soon. I hope it isn't at night, though. I flew for about half an hour this morning. The French coast was as plain as Punch.

We each have our own machines at last. Mine is the actual machine that Sippe [S.V. Sippe, D.S.O., Squadron Comdr., R.N.] had on his stunt to Friedrichshafen. Our chances of getting out to the front are remoter than ever, and each of these silly raids puts us further back still. If old Rumpler [the German airman] hadn't taken it into his head to drop a bomb on Dover on Xmas day, we should in all probability have been over the other side by now.

22nd January, 1915.

There has been a bit of a scare on today, but it has resulted as usual

THE FAMOUS 873 AVRO BIPLANE

FLOWN BY FLT.-COMM. S.V. SIPPE, D.S.O., IN THE RAID ON FRIEDERICHSHAFEN, AND BY FLT.-LIEUT. ROSHER IN THE TWO BIG RAIDS ON OSTENDE AND IN HIS RAID WITH MAJOR CORTNEY ON HOBO-KEN. THE MACHINE SURVIVED TO BE RETURNED TO ENGLAND FOR SCHOOL WORK. SHE IS HERE SHOEN ON THE POINT OF STARTING FOR FRIEDERICHSHAFEN.

in nothing, except that I missed my lunch. I quite enjoyed my patrol though. I was up an hour and twenty minutes and pottered around Deal. My beat was from the South to North Foreland and back. It was rather thick up [in the air], but I had an excellent view of Margate, Ramsgate, etc. I kept at about 4,000 feet. It was a bit cold, but not so bad as I expected.

28th January, 1915.

We all took the air at once today for the Admiral's benefit; quite a fine display.

No. 1 Aeroplane Squadron, Dover.
4th February, 1915.

We have four young marine officers just joined up with the Squadron to act as observers—rather a good idea, but they had a somewhat rough initiation this morning. Just after I had been enlarging to them on the safety of flying nowadays, there was a damned awful smash. An Avro came down in a nose dive from 400 feet.

There wasn't much left of it and the occupants were very lucky not being done in. B—— was pilot and came out with a badly sprained ankle, cuts, bruises and shock; and S——, the observer, who was in front, broke his right arm above the elbow and dislocated his hip, besides cuts, etc. I was in the air at the time, with Riggall as my passenger. He saw the accident, but I didn't know of it until I got down. B—— is our flight commander, so I suppose our move is once more indefinitely postponed.

I am putting in for leave this weekend, and think I shall get it with luck. Am just getting rid of an awful cold. Riggall and Maude [J. D. Maude, Flt. Comdr., R.N.] are both pretty rocky too—sort of flu or something.

Am enclosing a photo of my machine [Avro] 873. I think I told you it was the one Sippe used on his raid [on Friedrichshafen]. The one next it, [Avro] 875, is Babington's [J. T. Babington, D.S.O., Squadron Comdr., R.N.], and the next belonged to Briggs [E. F. Briggs, D.S.O., Squadron Comdr., R.N.] who was captured [in the raid].

9th February, 1915.

We had an old seaplane wrecked outside the harbour yesterday. The engine failed and a destroyer went out to tow the machine in. Unfortunately, the sea was rough and the destroyer rolled into the thing, damaging it so badly that it eventually sank. The pilot and passenger were taken off safely. It was quite interesting, watching from the top of the cliffs through glasses.

Love to all at home.

Ever your loving son,

Harold.

3
Raids on the Belgian Coast

12

To his Father

No. 1 Aeroplane Squadron,
Hotel Burlington, Dover.
12th February, 1915.

Dear Dad,

I wrote home last on Wednesday, and, as you no doubt guessed, there has since been something on. I could not, of course, let you know, as our success or otherwise depended greatly on secrecy. Wednesday was a very busy day. I tested my machine for half an hour in the morning, and by the evening everything was in tip-top running order. During the day . . . machines arrived from Hendon, Eastchurch, etc., etc., also . . . seaplanes turned up. Among the Hendon crowd was Grahame-White and one or two others I knew.

Thursday morning we were up betimes, and the weather being good, the D.A.D. [Commodore Murray F. Sueter, C.B., R.N., Director of Air Department] decided we should start. We had fixed up our maps, etc., overnight; my orders were to drop all my bombs on Zebrugge. It was a bit misty over the Channel, and I was one of the last to get away. We went in order—slowest machines first, at two-minute intervals. I pushed off just after 8 a.m., climbed to 2,000 feet and streaked off over the Channel. We had four destroyers at intervals across the Channel in case our engines went wrong, also seaplanes. It was mighty comforting to see them below. I got my first shock on looking at my rev. [revolution] counter, which was jumping from 950 to 1,200, when it should have been steady at 1,150. The machine was, however, pulling well, so I didn't worry.

In due course I struck Calais and headed up the coast about seven miles out to sea. I passed Gravelines and Dunkirk where I had reached 6,500 feet. Then a huge bank of black clouds loomed ahead. Our orders were to land at Dunkirk if clouds were too bad, but as two machines sogged on ahead of me, I pushed on too. It started with a thin mist and then gradually got thicker. I continued so for about ten minutes, and then found that, according to my compass, I had turned completely round and was heading out to sea. The clouds got thicker and the compass became useless, swinging round and round. I was about 7,000 feet up and absolutely lost. The next thing I realised was that my speed indicator had rushed up to 90 *miles* an hour and the wind was fairly whistling through the wires. I pulled her up, but had quite lost control.

A hair raising experience followed. I nose-dived, side-slipped, stalled,[1] etc., etc., time after time, my speed varying from practically nothing to over 100 miles an hour. I kept my head, but was absolutely scared stiff. I didn't get out of the clouds, which lower down turned into a snow-storm and hail, until I was only 1,500 feet up. I came out diving headlong for the earth. As soon as I saw the ground, I of course adjusted my sense of balance, and flattened out. I was, however, hopelessly lost. The sea was nowhere in sight, and, so far as I could judge, I was somewhere over our own line behind Nieuport.

I steered by my compass (which had recovered, being out of the clouds) and after a short time picked up the coast. I then tried to skirt round the snowstorm inland, but it went too far. Next I tried to get along the coast underneath the storm, but also failed at this, so, feeling awfully sick, I started back for Dunkirk, fully expecting to be the one failure of the party. On arrival there, however, I found them all back but one, and all had had similar experiences. One man turned completely upside down in the storm.

By the way, what finally decided me to come back was this. After trying to get under the storm along the coast (I had got very low down, about 3,000 feet), I heard two or three bangs, but took no notice. I happened to look round, however, and saw three nice little puffs of smoke about 100 yards behind me. Then came another, much nearer. "Shrapnel," says I, and off I went to Dunkirk.

---

1. Nose-diving, making a vertical descent. Side-slipping may occur to a machine that has lost her flying speed, and always occurs if the bank is too great or too little when turning. Stalling, loss of flying speed.

I was pretty cold on arrival, having been two hours in the air. Grahame-White came down in the sea and was picked up by one of our destroyers. Pottered round the aerodrome for a bit, and looked at French and Belgian machines. Anthony Wilding [2] is stationed there, also Carpentier,[3] whom I didn't see.

Motored into the town for lunch and had a look around. Out to the aerodrome again in the afternoon, but nothing doing. Slept on the *Empress* overnight. We first lay down on the couches in the saloon, then turned in at 11 p.m., awfully tired. At 3.0 a.m. the stewards came in to lay breakfast. At 5.30 we were all up, still tired, dirty, and feeling rotten. Motored out to the aerodrome in the dark, awfully cold, ugh! I was one of the first off (in the dark). I didn't relish it a tiny bit. The weather was misty and cloudy, and very cold. Off Nieuport I was five miles out to sea and 4,000 feet up. Before I came abreast of it, I saw flashes along the coast. A few seconds later, bang! bang! and the shrapnel burst a good deal short of me, but direction and height perfect. I turned out to sea and put another two miles between me and the coast. By now a regular cannonade was going on. All along the coast the guns were firing, nasty vicious flashes, and then a puff of smoke as the shrapnel burst. I steered a zigzag course and made steadily out to sea, climbing hard.

The clouds now became very troublesome. Ostend was simply a mass of guns. After flying for three-quarters of an hour, I reached Zebrugge. I had to come down to 5,500 feet because of the clouds. I streaked in through them, loosed my bombs, and then made off. I was hopelessly lost, and my performance of the day before was repeated in the clouds. I got clear, however, at 4,000 feet, heading straight out to sea and side-slipping hard, the earth appearing all sideways on. I fairly streaked out to sea, and then headed straight home. I got back after 1½ hours in the air.

As to what happened generally, I can't tell. It may possibly appear in the papers. Maude came down in the sea and was picked up. I got back here shortly after 4.0 p.m. by boat. Am bringing my machine back later, I expect. I thought of wiring you to come down for the night, but find it's not feasible. After all, Dover isn't such a bad place, I'm thinking. I don't mind owning that I have been scared stiff once or twice in the last two days. They are hitting with shrapnel at 8,000 feet.

2. The Tennis Champion, killed in action 12th May, 1915.
3. Georges Carpentier, the boxer, French airman, injured in an aeroplane accident, 12th August, 1915.

They reckon to get third shot on for a cert. One machine came back riddled with bullets. The pilot had got down to 450 feet in the mist.

With the very best love to all at home.

Ever your loving son,

Harold.

Note

The following is the Admiralty's official account of the raid described in the foregoing letters:—

During the last twenty-four hours, combined aeroplane and seaplane operations have been carried out by the Naval Wing in the Bruges, Zeebrugge, Blankenberghe and Ostend districts, with a view to preventing the develop ment of submarine bases and establishments.

Thirty-four naval aeroplanes and seaplanes took part.

Great damage is reported to have been done to Ostend Railway Station, which, according to present information, has probably been burnt to the ground. The railway station at Blankenberghe was damaged and railway lines were torn up in many places. Bombs were dropped on gun positions at Middelkerke, also on the power station and German mine-sweeping vessels at Zeebrugge, but the damage done is unknown.

During the attack the machines encountered heavy banks of snow.

No submarines were seen.

Flight Commander Grahame-White fell into the sea off Nieuport and was rescued by a French vessel.

Although exposed to heavy gunfire from rifles, anti-aircraft guns, *mitrailleuses*, etc., all pilots are safe. Two machines were damaged.

The seaplanes and aeroplanes were under the command of Wing Commander Samson, assisted by Wing Commander Longmore and Squadron Commanders Porte, Courtney, and Rathbone.

Harold Rosher went back to France on 13th February, 1915, and three days later took part in a further great raid, of winch the following is the Admiralty's official account:—

The air operations of the Naval Wing against the Bruges, Ostend-Zeebrugge District have been continued.

This afternoon 40 aeroplanes and seaplanes bombarded Ostend,

FLIGHT-LIEUT. HAROLD ROSHER, R.N.

Middelkerke, Ghistelles, and Zeebrugge.

Bombs were dropped on the heavy batteries situated on the east and west sides of Ostend harbour; on the gun position at Middelkerke; on transport waggons on the Ostend-Ghistelles road; on the mole at Zeebrugge to widen the breach damaged in former attacks; on the locks at Zeebrugge; on barges outside Blankenberghe, and on trawlers outside Zeebrugge.

Eight French aeroplanes assisted the naval machines by making a vigorous attack on the Ghistelles aerodrome, thus effectively preventing the German aircraft from cutting off our machines. It is reported that good results were obtained.

Instructions are always issued to confine the attacks to points of military importance, and every effort is made by the flying officers to avoid dropping bombs on any residential portions of the towns.

Air Raid, 16th February, 1915.—Harold Rosher sent no written account of this raid, as he returned to Dover immediately after taking part in it. Describing his experiences in the raid, he stated that his instructions were to drop his bombs on a certain place behind Ostend. On leaving Dunkirk he flew up the coast. When he got past Nieuport, he came under heavy fire, and headed out to sea. Off Ostend the firing was terrific, and seeing ahead a big bank of clouds he continued past Ostend until he got above them. Thus concealed he turned and came inland, and was able to reach his objective unobserved. The explosion of his bombs was the first intimation the enemy had of his presence. Anti-aircraft batteries immediately opened fire on him, but by that time he was making off, and flying some miles out to sea, he came back down the coast in safety to Dunkirk. One can imagine the strained anxiety with which those who come back from raids such as this, await the arrival of overdue comrades. On this occasion three of them, including Harold's special chum, Flight-Lt. Gordon Riggall, never returned.

13

TO HIS FATHER

Hotel Burlington, Dover.
24th February, 191 5.

Dear Dad,

I arrived here safely in excellent time after quite a comfy journey. Mr. and Mrs. Riggall left yesterday, but during the course of the afternoon I received a very nice letter from him . . . [Their son, Lieut. Riggall, was "missing"].

If you can possibly manage it, come down tomorrow (Thursday) night. In case I am unable to meet you at the station, come straight on to the Burlington. I will reserve you a room. The Dunkirk boat was missed twice by torpedoes yesterday. She is now running very irregularly. I cannot be certain as to my movements, but will put you off by wire if necessary. On arrival here I found all my letters had been forwarded to the other side, also my Gieve lifebelt. . . .

I think I just got away from home before you all quite spoilt me. It's awfully bad for one, you know, and mustn't occur again or I shall be getting quite beyond myself. I thoroughly enjoyed every moment of my leave (except the being "shown off" part, which I endured with as good grace as possible), but I don't want anyone to run away with the idea that I have done anything extraordinary. One has only to go across the other side to realise that everybody out there is doing his best. Army pilots are flying day after day for hours on end, under fire, and trench life must be no less trying. After all, when one comes to think of it, it was what I joined the Air Service for, and probably when all is said and done, the everyday routine will prove a much tougher job than these occasional stunts.

Well, I've gassed long enough, so goodbye and very best love to all at home (mind you come down tomorrow night unless I wire you otherwise) .

Ever your loving son,
Harold.

P.S.—The watch is keeping excellent time and the pipe is settling down into first-rate smoking order.

4

With the B.E.F.

TO HIS MOTHER

No. 1 Naval Aeroplane Squadron, B.E.F.
1st March, 1915.

Dearest Mum,

I only had time to scrawl off a few lines to you this morning, as the mail was just going out. We have been pretty busy the last day or so getting things shipshape. I am at last settled in a quite nice house with seven others. Maude and I are the two senior inmates, so are running the establishment. Unfortunately, we have no bath, but five minutes' walk from here there are some public baths, where we can get a hot tub any time between 8 a.m. and 7 p.m.

We are acting as our own censors here, and also have to censor all the men's letters—some of them are most amusing. There is nothing exciting at all happening. Weather has been pretty bad and shows signs of getting worse.

Have just run out of ink, am now writing with coffee!

4th March, 1915.

We are settling down by degrees. Our house is really beginning to get quite comfortable. Wilding has been staying here with us the last few days.

6th March, 1915.

Had my first letter from you this morning, dated the 3rd, for which many thanks. It's the first news of any sort from home since we have been out here. Weather still continues very bad and, personally, I shouldn't mind a little more of it still.

Did I tell you that my Gieve lifebelt had turned up? You can't imagine how firmly attached I am to it. I can't bear parting with it at night. The flask I have filled up to the stopper with rum—brandy and whisky are unprocurable.

We don't get much in the way of light literature, so any weekly papers, such as *Sketches, Tatters, Punch,* are looked on as great luxuries. By the way, is the watch keeping good time? I had the chance of being inoculated the other day, but didn't think it worthwhile. I may be done later, possibly.

Ever your loving son. Love to all at home.

Harold.

P.S.—There is a rumour that we get a week's leave after being out here three months.

15

To his Mother

No. 1 Aeroplane Squadron, B.E.F.
7th March, 1915.

Dearest Mum,

Have just got your letter of the 4th inst. It arrived late in the day, after Dad's. I am afraid this has missed the mail; so won't go off for a couple of days. I have just come off duty; we get three days at it on end. There's no baccy to be procured out here, so could you send me on a ½ lb. tin of Friars' Mixture (medium)?

Am just back from a little bomb-dropping stunt over Ostend, but keep it quiet until it appears in the papers, or if it doesn't, allow say a week. It was bitterly cold and took about 1½ hours.

I pushed the old bus up to 8,000 ft., right above a terrific layer of clouds. It was a most wonderful sight. I only got occasional glimpses of the earth and sea, and was not fired at at all—in fact, I don't think I was ever even seen.

It's quite impossible for me to let you know my whereabouts in France, but I seem to have a vague recollection of telling you where I was going before I left. If you can remember, all well and good. If not, put two and two together, and the answer is ——?

Heaps of love to all, and Cheer O! for my week's leave in 3 months' time.

Ever your loving son,
Harold.

Note

The following is the Admiralty's official account of the raid de-

42

scribed in the foregoing letter:—

Wing Commander Longmore reports that an air attack on Ostend was carried out yesterday afternoon (7th March) by six aeroplanes of the Naval Wing. Of these two had to return owing to petrol freezing.

The remainder reached Ostend and dropped eleven bombs on the submarine repair base and four bombs on the Kursaal, the headquarters of the military.

All machines and pilots returned.

It is probable that considerable damage was done. No submarines were seen in the basin.

The attack was carried out in a fresh N.N.W. wind.

16
TO HIS FATHER

No. 1 Aeroplane Squadron, B.E.F.
8th March, 1915.

Dear Dad,

I have struck rather an unfortunate day today. To begin with, this morning I was taxying my machine to the far end of the aerodrome, to start off into the wind, when I got into some very soft ground—result, before I knew where I was, I found the machine standing up on its nose. Fortunately, the only damage was a broken propeller, which didn't matter, as it was already chipped and was going to be replaced. In the afternoon I had quite a good trip, just over an hour, and quite long enough, as it has been pretty nearly freezing all day long. I made a good landing, but a second or so after I actually touched the ground, a tyre burst, and I all but turned a complete somersault. For several seconds I was quite vertical, and then the machine fell back. One or two things were bent, but on the whole remarkably little damage. The skid broke and leading edge of one wing tip. A wheel also buckled up, but I should be going strong again by tomorrow.

12th March, 1915.

Still going strong and things on the whole keeping fairly quiet. There has been another little bomb-dropping episode, in which I didn't take part, however, as my machine was undergoing some repairs. Please send on my fur coat at once, as my leather one has given out suddenly—am sending it back to Gieve's immediately on receipt of other.

14th March, 1915.

Many thanks for letter. Flight, and the *Aeroplane*, received yesterday. The days are lengthening out tremendously now, and we manage to get in quite a good walk after tea along the front. There is an excellent promenade, crowded with the town folk, and most gorgeous sands with heaps of very pretty shells. The sands make a most perfect landing ground and have already come in very useful in emergency.

I flew a Vickers gun bus [gun-carrying biplane] the other day (you saw one at Dover, I think), I didn't like it much. For one thing it was very badly balanced, and secondly, I don't like a monosoupape [engine] (100 h.p. Gnome).

My own machine I can get so perfectly balanced that I can let go the controls for minutes on end. Had a delightful trip today to ... It's most interesting watching the shells burst. Somebody's beginning to push pretty hard in places, I can tell you. We hear the guns hammering away day and night now.

Our aerodrome here is a beastly small one. I have had several narrow shaves already of running into things, and feel sure that before long I shall "crash" something. I think that I shall shortly have an opportunity of flying a monoplane. Am looking forward to it "some."

Love to all.

Ever your loving son,
Harold.

17

To his Mother

No. 1 Naval Aeroplane Squadron, B.E.F.
15th March, 1915.

Dearest Mum,

Have had a great time today. First thing in the morning the C.O. gave Maude and myself the whole day off. We promptly secured a car, passports and passwords, had an early lunch, and then sallied forth full of hope to see the War. Our password held good until we got into Belgium, and then proved "dud." The sentry, however, very kindly supplied us with another. We were rather unfortunate in getting a tyre punctured, but half a dozen Belgian soldiers rushed up and asked us if we wanted any help, and how many men. They carefully explained they would do anything to help the English. Eventually they did everything for us. The place we visited was the same as I went to when over here before.

This afternoon it was being rather heavily bombarded. We left our car outside the town, shells bursting within 50 yards of it. We then sallied forth on foot into the town—terrific bangs from the French guns firing near us, and shells fairly whistling overhead. You can tell when they are coming near you by the sound they make.

The French soldiers are quite wily, and scuttle away like rabbits, when they hear one coming near. In the town several shells burst very near us, and fragments of stone and dust fell freely around us—rather too warm for my liking. There was quite a difference since I was last there, several more buildings being reduced to ruins. One shell hole would have concealed 40 or 50 men easily. We only stayed half an hour, and saw quite enough.

Two Frenchmen were killed here this evening. They stalled and side-slipped from about 80 feet in a Voisin and were killed instantly. From what I heard they were smashed to bits.

It's all luck. B—— fell 400 feet and only sprained his ankle, and these two fellows broke every bone in their bodies. The machine caught fire on the ground and was burnt to bits. I saw the remains this evening.

Two French machines and four pilots are missing from a little bomb-dropping stunt of theirs yesterday. You never hear of these things at home, but flying casualties are heavier than one is led to believe. A short time back the R.F.C. [Royal Flying Corps] lost five in a week!

Have just discovered that the Duchess of Sutherland and Lady Rosemary are running a hospital out here.

French sanitary arrangements are really extraordinary. I don't believe there is a drain in the place. Such things are unknown in small French towns.

Am sending you a cheque for £20, as it is an awful nuisance getting cash here. I want you to send me on £5 at once in notes and the rest as I ask, as I don't want a lot of money about me.

Also I expect I owe you something for flea bag, etc., and I am sure to be wanting other things later. Am sending you on the pins and brooches.

Very best love.

Ever your loving son,
Harold.

18

To his Mother

No. 1 Naval Aeroplane Squadron, B.E.F.
16th March, 1915.

Dearest Mum,

Whatever induced you to do it? The tobacco, etc., arrived, but the toffee had all melted, and a more sticky mess you can't conceive. It was as much as I could do to read your letter. I managed to rescue some of the toffee and the general opinion on same is that it is very good. Two letters from Dad and the sleeping bag arrived by same mail, for which many thanks.

I had to make a hurried landing on the sands today owing to an exhaust cam [valve operating mechanism] breaking. Flew my machine back in the evening. Have just started another three days' duty.

Love to all.

Ever your loving son,
Harold.

19

To his Father

No. 1 Naval Aeroplane Squadron, B.E.F.
21st March, 1915.

Dear Dad,

Very little news of interest to tell you. I was sent out suddenly yesterday afternoon late to look for a Zepp, but saw nothing. It was dusk by the time I got back, and an inlet valve went just as I was coming in. I couldn't reach our aerodrome, but just managed to scrape into the Belgian one alongside. The French brought down a Taube today and one yesterday (anti-aircraft guns). They are getting nearly as hot as the Germans. I can tell you that some of us are beginning to think our chances of seeing England again are somewhat remote.

Today has been the most perfect day we have had out here so far. This afternoon I shot a wild duck with a Webley-Scott pistol at 50 yards. It was the 6th shot, but the others were all very close—not bad shooting, eh?

The *Punches* turned up alright, but much later than the other papers—all much appreciated. Best love.

Ever your loving son,
Harold.

20

TO HIS MOTHER.

No. 1 Squadron, R.N.A.S., B.E.F.
23rd March, 1915.

Dearest Mum,

Another fine day, and let's hope the weather will last. The town this afternoon is crowded with small girls all in white—long skirts and veils—confirmation, I suppose.

Have spent a very busy day tuning up my bus, and am not over satisfied with it now. Tomorrow at the crack of dawn I am off on another stunt, this time more hazardous than ever. When I start thinking of the possibilities, or rather probabilities, I go hot and cold by turns; so endeavour to switch off on to something else, but it keeps coming back to the same old thing. Am not posting this until just before I start, but all the same can tell you no details.

By the time you get this, I shall either have returned safely or be elsewhere. The papers will no doubt give you more news than I can at present. Suffice it to say, that my journey will be round about 200 miles and will last 4—5 hours. It is even doubtful whether we shall have enough petrol to bring us back. It's a first-rate stunt though, and I suppose a feather in my cap, being one of the chosen few. Very best love to all.

Ever your loving son,
Harold.

21

TO HIS MOTHER AND FATHER

No. 1 Squadron, R.N.A.S., B.E.F.
24th March, 1915,

Dearest Mum and Dad,

Another successful little jaunt. Five of us were chosen to go—Capt. Courtney [Major Ivor T. Courtney, Squadron Comdr., R.N.], Meates (who travelled up to town from Dover in the train with Dad) self, and two subs named Andreae and Huskisson. Courtney and I got there and back, Meates [B. C, Flt. Lieut. R.N.] came down in Holland with engine trouble, and is interned. . . . Andreae [P. G. Andreae, Flt. Lieut., R.N.] lost his way in the clouds and fog, and came back, and Huskisson [B. L. Huskisson, Flt. Comdr., R.N.] did the same, only dropped his bombs on Ostend on the way. Our mark, by the way, was the submarine base at Hoboken, near Antwerp.

Yesterday morning we were to have gone, but the weather was not good enough, and last night we slept at the aerodrome, so as to get off at the "crack of dawn." This morning we got up about 3.30 a.m. (thank goodness, the weather was warm), and breakfast followed. It's mighty hard to get down eggs and bread and butter at that hour. We cut for the order of starting, but decided to keep as near one another as possible. I went off last but one, at 5.30 a.m., and streaked out straight across the sea. We were pretty heavily loaded, and my bus wouldn't climb much. I saw one machine ahead of me, but lost it almost immediately in the clouds, which were very low (2,500 feet), and it was also very misty.

Our course was right up the coast, past Zeebrugge, and then cut in across the land. At the mouth of the Scheldt I got clear of some of the clouds and saw Courtney behind and 2,000 feet above me, my machine then being about 5,000 feet only. He rapidly overtook me (we were all on Avros, but his was faster), and from then on I followed him over the clouds. Unfortunately, over Antwerp there were no clouds. Courtney was about five or six minutes in front of me, and I saw him volplane out of sight. I had to go on some little way before I spotted the yards myself. I next saw Courtney very low down, flying away to the coast with shrapnel bursting around him. He came down to under 500 feet, and being first there, dropped his bombs before he was fired on.

As the wind was dead against me, I decided to come round in a semi-circle to cross the yards with the wind, so as to attain a greater speed. I was only 5,500 feet up, and they opened fire on me with shrapnel as soon as I got within range. It began getting a bit hot, so before I got quite round I shut off my petrol, and came down with a steep volplane until I was 2,500 feet, when I turned on my petrol again, and continued my descent at a rate of well over a hundred miles an hour. I passed over the yards at about 1,000 feet only, and loosed all my bombs over the place. The whole way down I was under fire, two anti-aircraft in the yard, guns from the forts on either side, rifle fire, *mitrailleuse* or machine guns, and, most weird of all, great bunches (15 to 20) of what looked like green rockets, but I think they were flaming bullets.

The excitement of the moment was terrific. I have never travelled so fast before in my life. My first impressions were the great speed, the flaming bullets streaking by, the incessant rattle of the machine gun and rifle fire, and one or two shells bursting close by, knocking my

SQUADRON-COMMANDER IVOR T. COURTNEY, R.N. (MAJOR R.M.L I.), WHO LED THE RAID ON HOBOKEN, DESCRIBED IN THE ACCOMPANYING LETTER.

machine all sideways, and pretty nearly deafening me.

On my return I found my machine was only hit twice—rather wonderful; one bullet hole through the tail and a piece of shrapnel buried in the main spar of one wing. I have now got it out.

I found myself across the yards, and felt a mild sort of surprise. My eyes must have been sticking out of my head like a shrimp's! I know I was gasping for breath and crouching down in the fuselage [body of the machine]. I was, however, by no means clear, for shrapnel was still bursting around me. I jammed the rudder first one way and then the other. I banked first on one wing tip, and then on to the other, now slipping outwards, and now up and now down. I was literally hedged in by forts (and only 1,000 feet up), and had to run the gauntlet before getting away. I was under rifle fire right up to the frontier, and even then the Dutch potted me.

My return journey was trying. Most of the time I had to fly at under 500 feet, as I ran into thick clouds and mist. I pottered gaily right over Flushing, and within a few hundred yards of a Dutch cruiser and two torpedo boats. I got back home about a quarter of an hour after Courtney, having been very nearly four hours in the air, and having covered, I suppose, getting on for 250 miles.

Have not yet heard what damage was done. The C.O. was awfully braced.

I had some breakfast when I got back, wrote out my report, had lunch, and then a very, very hot bath. Tomorrow I am going out with Courtney to see the War, as we have been given the day off to do as we please.

My engine gave me several anxious moments. For some reason it cut right out over the Scheldt, and I had actually given up all hope when it picked up again. It was pretty risky work flying several miles out to sea, only just in sight of land too, but our surprise (or I should say Courtney's) of the Germans was certainly complete.

Must really stop now.

Ever your loving son,
Harold.

Note

The following is the Admiralty's official account of the Antwerp raid:—

The Secretary of the Admiralty yesterday afternoon [24th March] issued the following communication from Wing Commander Longmore:—

I have to report that a successful air attack was carried out this morning by five machines of the Dunkirk Squadron on the German submarines being constructed at Hoboken near Antwerp.

Two of the pilots had to return owing to thick weather, but Squadron Commander Ivor T. Courtney and Flight Lieutenant H. Rosher reached their objective, and after planing down to 1000 feet dropped four bombs each on the submarines. It is believed that considerable damage has been done to both the works and to submarines. The works were observed to be on fire. In all five submarines were observed on the slip.

Flight Lieutenant B. Crossley-Meates was obliged by engine trouble to descend in Holland.

Owing to the mist the two pilots experienced considerable difficulty in finding their way, and were subjected to a heavy gun-fire while delivering their attack.

The French official *communiqué* gave precise details, thus:—

At Hoboken the Antwerp shipbuilding yard was set on fire and two submarines were destroyed, while a third was damaged. Forty German workmen were killed and sixty-two wounded.

22
To his Father

No. 1 Squadron, R.N.A.S., B.E.F.
26th March, 1915.

Dear Dad,

I had quite a good time yesterday with Courtney, although the weather was so bad. We started out gaily through Bergues, a ripping little town, then Cassel, a most delightful spot. It is perched up on a hill in the middle of a plain and you get a grand view around. We visited some R.F.C. people at St. Omer, had lunch there and then went out to Wipers (Ypres). There was nothing doing there, but even though we had all sorts of passes, we could not get near the firing line. The Cloth Hall and Cathedral we thoroughly inspected though—most lovely places, utterly in ruins. The remainder of the town is really very little touched—nothing like Nieuport, where there is not a whole building anywhere.

We got back home about 6 p.m., having enjoyed ourselves immensely and feeling quite tired out. My troubles weren't over though, as I found a little "chit" awaiting me, asking me to dine with the Commander.

The First Lord wired his "Congrats" to us through Longmore—some feather in our caps, what! This morning I see all sorts of garbled accounts in the newspapers. My photo in the ———— is awful. ————ought to be shot.

Must close as the mail is just going out. Best love to all.

Ever your loving son,

Harold.

23

TO HIS MOTHER

No. 1 Squadron, R.N.A.S., B.E.F.
31st March, 1915.

Dearest Mum,

We can hear the guns when the wind is our way, and on a clear day we can see shrapnel bursting in the air. What do you think of this story, the latest from the trenches? It's not quite a drawing-room one!

One Tommy, speaking to another over the trenches:—"'Ello, Bill, got a lice over there?"

"Garn, we ain't lousy."

"I mean a boot-lice."

Love to all.

Ever your loving son,

Harold.

P.S.—Meates did get to Hoboken and came down in Holland on return journey.

Tell Dad to let me know when he is coming, as near as possible, so that perhaps I can arrange to meet him. The boat does not cross here every day, but he can also come *via* Calais. Think I can fix up a room over the road.

24

TO HIS SISTER

No. 1 Squadron, R.N.A.S., B.E.F.
1st April, 1915.

Dear old Girl,

I really feel I owe you a few lines, as you have honoured me with several epistles lately, which I fear have remained unanswered.

Did my last letter to Mother arrive very sticky? It left here sopping wet, and thereby hangs a tale. I hadn't time to re-write it, as the mail was just going out. I unfortunately had the letter on me and, in conjunction with myself, it got rather a bad ducking.

I was sent up with an observer this morning in a Vickers gun bus (a pusher machine), and all went well until coming home, when my engine petered out, when I was only 400 feet over the town. I hadn't much choice of landing grounds, and preferred to come down in one of the docks to landing on a housetop or in a maze of telegraph wires. I pancaked [flattened out] as much as possible, but hit the water with a bit of a biff. Things then began to happen pretty suddenly. I remember seeing my observer shot out into the water about twenty yards ahead, and the next thing I knew was that I was under the water and still in the machine.

I was scared "some," and the water tasted beastly salt, but I pulled myself together, and says I to myself, ses I, "Harold, my boy, if you don't keep your head and get out of this damn quick, you'll drown for a cert like a rat in a trap." So I carefully thought out just where the top plane would be, and disentangled myself from things in general. It took a long time though, and I was relieved "some" when I bobbed up to the surface. I was rather surprised at keeping afloat very easily, as I had heaps of clothes on.

On arrival at the surface, I found my observer hanging on to the machine, and it didn't take me long to get a hold on it myself. We were only about 40 yards from the side of the dock, but didn't venture to swim, as the sides were twenty feet high, and the ladders only just reached to the water. There were no boats at all there, but we soon had a hundred or so dock hands around the side, all of whom seemed to talk very volubly, but were very incompetent.

The water was icy cold and we were very cold before coming into it. With some difficulty I managed to undo a button or so and blow out my Gieves waistcoat, but it wasn't really necesary as I was keeping afloat well.

After a bit some life belts were thrown out, and two men came out on a little raft. I swam to a lifebelt and my observer (Collen) [Lieut. A. R. Col- len, R.M.A.] got on the raft. We both had to be hauled up out of the dock with ropes, and by the time we got on *terra firma*, it was as much as we could do to stand up. We were in the water about 20 minutes, and I don't think I have ever been so cold before.

We walked rapidly off to the aerodrome, half a mile away, and

ONE VICKERS FIGHTING BIPLANE PHOTOGRAPHED BY ANOTHER

A VICKERS FIGHTING BIPLANE
IT WAS ON A MACHINE OF THIS TYPE THAT LIEUT. ROSHER PLUNGED
INTO THE DOCKS AT DUNKIRK

there had a stiff rum and milk, and stripped in front of a fire and had a good rub down. We had lunch wrapped up in towels and were then rigged out in blue jerseys and blue serge trousers. This afternoon we have both had a hot bath and are feeling none the worse. The C.O. was very amused about the whole proceeding and laughed heartily at us. The machine is but very little damaged, but will take some salving. My pocket book, cheque book, etc., are all in a nasty sticky state. Thank goodness! I hadn't my gold watch. My clothes (including new fur coat) are, I am afraid, all ruined.

This afternoon Garros [Lieut. Roland Garros] shot down a Taube from his Morane. The poor wretches were burnt to death. Two of our people raided Zeebrugge and Hoboken again this morning.

Love to all.

Ever your loving brother,
Harold.

25

To his Father

No. 1, Naval Aeroplane Squadron, B.E.F.,
12th April, 1915.

Dear Dad,

Many thanks for letter received yesterday telling of your safe return. I think you must have omitted enclosure. By the way, the papers turned up the day after you left.

Have been very busy the last two days with our new busses. None have been flown yet, but we are prepared for fireworks. Three men have been killed on them in Paris in the last month. Babington and Sippe are both back. S—— G—— turned base over apex on landing his tabloid [fast scouting machine].

15th April, 1915.

Sad to relate, I have decided to part with old 873. She was really getting too ancient, and has now been packed up and is going to be sent home for School work; too bad, isn't it? It would have been a far better ending had I crashed her. I have written up her raids in- side the fuselage—(1) Friedrichshafen, (2) Zeebrugge, (3) Ostend, (4) Ostend again, and (5) Hoboken—some record! I asked permission to fly her home, but the C.O. didn't bite. I was awfully disappointed.

My new bus is a Morane parasol, 80 h.p. Le Rhone. They are supposed to climb like fire and do over 80 miles per hour, but are very touchy on the elevator and rather trying to fly. I have not yet been up in her.

Garros brought another machine down today, and a Frenchman managed to fly back to our own lines after having one foot smashed by shrapnel over Ostend.

17th April, 1915.

Very little news of interest to tell you, but here goes for what there is. My Morane parasol was ready today and Babington tested it. If the weather is fine tomorrow, I shall float forth on it into the "ethereal blue." Not having flown a monoplane before, I am all of a "doo-da."

Yesterday I went out to see the War at N——. Though a fine day, the Bosches were not bombarding, so we went around in peace, and I brought back a few shell fragments with me which you may find interesting. For the rest, our miserable lives continue much as before. The Frenchmen here have lost a machine today, but the R.F.C. brought down an Aviatik at Wipers, so that makes us all square.

19th April, 1915.

I have flown my Morane twice. It is a most comic affair, but I think I shall like it when I get more used to it. It is very light on the controls, especially the elevator, and gets off the ground before you can say "squeak." Garros was missing last night, and there has since been a rumour that he is a prisoner of war.[1] This is, of course, a nasty knock for us.

A Frenchman had rather a bad accident here this morning. He ran over the bank at the top end of the aerodrome in a Voisin and turned a complete somersault. The machine immediately caught fire. The passenger got off all right, but the pilot was badly burnt. Five minutes after they got him out one of his bombs went off with a terrific bang. The machine was entirely wrecked.

24th April, 1915.

Just a few lines to let you know I am still in the land of the living. I see in the papers that Colonel Rosher (Dorsets) has been killed in the Persian Gulf. The Dorsets seem to have had a pretty rough time.

Spenser Grey [Squadron Commander Spenser D. A. Grey, D.S.O., R.N.] and Marsden [Flt. Lieut. H. S. Marsden, R.N.] paid a visit to Ostend today with bombs, and Sippe was turned upside down on the ground in a Morane by a gust of wind this afternoon. He was unhurt, but the machine was badly damaged.

---

1. Lieutenant-aviator Roland Garros (French) was forced to land near Ingelmunster, in West Flanders, on the evening of the 18th April, and was taken prisoner.

THE OVERTURNED MORANE
TO WHICH REFERENCE IS MADE IN THE
ACCOMPANYING NOTE. LIEUT. ROSHER WAS UNDER
THE MACHINE WHEN THE PHOTOGRAPH WAS TAKEN.

A SNAPSHOT OF LIEUT. ROSHER
TAKEN ABOUT THE PERIOD OF THE
ACCIDENT.

27th April, 1915.

Many thanks for the torches, papers, etc. There is nothing much doing here at the moment. According to the papers, the Germans are making another dash for this place. There is certainly a hell of a row going on. We hear the guns day and night.

29th April, 1915.

Not a line from anyone for quite three days! Whatever has become of you all? There has been some excitement here today. To begin with, three enemy aircraft came over here before breakfast, and then another between eleven and twelve o'clock. It was most comic to see our infuriated machines dashing off into the atmosphere in pursuit, with not an earthly chance of catching them. Soon after eleven o'clock there was a big explosion in the town and we all did a great leap into the air. From then, for nearly three hours, we were shelled with the greatest regularity at five minute intervals.

We all climbed on to the roof of one of our sheds and watched through glasses the explosions, occurring to the second almost; big stuff it was too, 12" I should say, and fired from the back of Nieuport, quite 20 miles away. The total bag was 40 killed and 60 wounded. They put about 20 shells into the town, one only 500 yards from the Sophie.[2] To give you an idea of the damage they do, one shell wrecked two houses entirely and half of both houses on either side. Windows were broken in the streets all round—"some" mess, I can tell you.

Love to all,

Ever your loving son,

Harold.

Note

About the end of April Lieut. Kosher crashed on his Morane at Dunkirk. The machine overturned and was completely smashed up, but he came out uninjured.

---

2. The villa where he was billeted.

5

Taking a New Machine to France

Note

In the second week of May, 1915, Harold Rosher arrived home unexpectedly, with orders to fly a new machine, a B.E. 2 C, from Hendon to Dunkirk. He tried the machine, but was not satisfied with the engine. On the 12th May, however, he telephoned to his father to come to the aerodrome to lunch with him, as he intended, if possible, to make a start immediately after lunch. The latter accordingly joined him, and about 3 p.m. Harold got into the machine and his father bade him farewell. As he rose, one could hear the engine missing, and at about 1000 feet, realising that there was clearly something wrong, Harold turned back to the aerodrome. Mechanics from the makers were sent for and they spent a day or two on the engine. On the 16th May, as he was told nothing more could be done to it, he decided to move of. He got across to Dunkirk, and his experiences *en route* are described in the following letters.

26

To his Mother

The Grand Hotel, Folkestone.
17th May, 1915.

Dearest Mum,

I was up betimes yesterday morning, but did not get away from Hendon until about 7.0 a.m. I could only secure half a dozen biscuits and a cup of tea before leaving. It was very thick, and clouds at 4,000 feet. I went *via* Harrow, Staines, and Redhill. Once at this last place, all you have to do is to follow the railway line, which runs straight as a die to Ashford. My engine was most alarming, making all sorts of weird noises, and I was kept very busy the whole way spotting the field I should land in if it petered out.

A pretty strong head wind made the going slow, and just after Redhill I ran into rain. I stuck it for half an hour, getting very wet and seeing hardly anything. Then the engine showed serious signs of giving up the ghost. What finally made me decide to come down was that I couldn't get any pressure in my petrol tank. I went on a bit and then chose a good-looking field with a road on one side and some houses at one corner. Here I landed in great style.

On getting down, the field was not quite so good as it looked from above, being on a slope and with a somewhat uneven surface. The usual crowd collected, despite the ram, and I soon had the machine covered up with tarpaulins and a territorial guard installed. I had breakfast with a Mr. and Mrs. R—— close by, and afterwards went into Headcorn, a mile away, and telephoned to the Admiralty, etc. I had lunch with the R——s and five daughters (swish, I was all of a doo-da!), and then spent the whole of the afternoon trying to get my beastly engine to go. It's an awful dud.

I eventually took the air before an admiring crowd at about 5.0 p.m., and made for Folkestone soon after. It was a wretched evening, and though it had stopped raining, I had to come down to under 2,000 feet to avoid clouds. I caught a glimpse of Wye when passing Ash- ford. Made a very stunt landing here and met a R.F.C. officer I know. We came straight on to the Grand, and after a drink at the Metropole, I had a bath, then dinner and a smoke, and went to bed. Today it is blowing a gale and raining cats and dogs. Am proceeding to Dover first opportunity.

Love to all.

Ever your loving son,
Harold.

27

To his Father

No. 1 Wing, R.N.A.S., B.E.F.
19th May, 1915.

Dear Dad,

I have at last arrived safely at my destination. Yesterday was a rotten day, but I motored to Dover in the afternoon and from there into St. Margaret's Bay, where I saw the holes made by the Zepp bombs. They were most disappointing, being very small, one foot by six inches deep. They were incendiary and not explosive.

I took the air from Folkestone this afternoon at 3.15 and circled round for 15 minutes, getting to only 2,000 feet. At that I pushed off across the Channel. My engine developed a most appalling vibration, and I hardly hoped to reach the other side. I arrived at Calais at 1,500 feet, and struggled on up the coast here.

Things are much as usual. I am taking an 80 Avro out to an advanced base tomorrow morning, the B.E., of course, being useless. Maude and Andreae are at Whale Island, the Commander in town, and Sippe and Wilson [J. P. Wilson, D.S.O., Squadron Comdr., R.N.] in Paris. We are all at the aerodrome and most uncomfy—Baillie [Lieut. J. E. Innes Baillie, R.M.A.] on leave, and Courtney going on sick leave tomorrow. Please send the gramophone at once.

21st May, 1915.

Here I am, going strong at our advanced base, only five miles behind the firing line. I was up yesterday morning at four, but did not get away in the Avro until five, as it was very misty. I arrived here in due course. We have a ripping little villa at ———. It is a most interesting place; the King of the Belgians lives here. We were shelled the night before last, and a Taube came over this morning and dropped a bomb at the end of the aerodrome. Will write more later.

22nd May, 1915.

Nothing very much in the way of news. A Taube came right over the aerodrome this morning at about 7,000 feet. I at once went after it in the Avro, but got nowhere near. First thing this morning I saw a Maurice coming down vertically and spinning hard—lost sight of it behind the housetops—pilot and passenger badly hurt—was surprised to hear they were alive. It was a horrid sight. Anxiously awaiting arrival of gramophone.

23rd May, 1915.

Turned out soon after five this morning and went up for an hour and a half waiting for Taubes. I chased several allied machines, but found nothing hostile. Had not been down twenty minutes before one came out. Later on in the morning two came right over the aerodrome. I went up in pursuit, but got nowhere near them. Things are pretty lively on the whole. Besides the regular artillery, there is an intermittent cannonade of anti-aircraft guns, either from us at the Taubes or from the Huns at us. The sky becomes absolutely dotted with little puffs of shrapnel, which are visible for half an hour at least.

This evening I went into the town. It's full of life, a band playing and all the shops open.

Babington flew my B.E. yesterday,[1] and the beastly thing nearly caught fire. We are getting a new engine for it from Paris.

Love to all.

Ever: your loving son,
Harold.

---

1. This was the machine he flew from Hendon to Dunkirk..

6

With the B.E.F. Again

28

To his Mother

No. 1 Wing, R.N.A.S., B. Squadron, B.E.F.
29th May, 1915.

Dearest Mum,

Have not written for ages, but you must excuse, as we have been so busy. This is really my first opportunity. All sorts of things have been happening. To begin with, the Commander announced the other night that the whole wing is going to be recalled within the next two months, so I shall anyhow be home again before long—expect to go into seaplanes.

We had a Zep scare the other night, though it was blowing half a gale. We were at the aerodrome all night, and went up at 3.0 a.m. for an hour and a half—eventually got to bed at 6.0 a.m. and slept until 10 o'clock.

We have been having some lovely weather lately, except the last few days, which have been bad. All the same we keep flying in any weather, sometimes two and three trips a day.

I went out to the War the other afternoon to see one of our anti-aircraft guns. We fired into the German trenches, and about two minutes later they replied with zest. Four or five shells whizzed over and burst about 30 yards behind us in a field. I picked up some fragments almost too hot to hold. We were within 1000 yards of the Huns and could see their and our own trenches rippingly through glasses.

Have given up chasing Taubes. One can never get them. We have commandeered an old bathing hut for our office at the aerodrome, and have rigged up an awning outside, and bought deckchairs. You should see us all lying back in the sun with field glasses glued to our eyes, watching the various aeroplanes, with shrapnel bursting all round them. Our shooting is awfully bad on the whole.

Our villa is first-rate, and oh! the gramophone has arrived safe and sound. Willing hands helped to unpack it, and we got it going in record time. It is immensely appreciated. We had some Belgian officers to dinner the other night, and last night we visited them. They are awfully good fellows and we got on famously. Last night was great fun.

The Belgian C—— had unfortunately swallowed two submarines by mistake, and the only English he knew was, "To your eyes." This we drank, also "England *toujours*" and "*Vive les Beiges.*" English and French songs were sung, etc., etc. There was a huge uproar. The Belgian C—— would insist on wearing B——'s hat, and bestowed many kisses on the badge before parting with it.

I do wish my camera would arrive, as I am missing some great opportunities.

Love to all.

Ever your loving son,
Harold.

29
TO HIS SISTER

No. 1 Wing, R.N.A.S.,
B. Squadron, B.E.F.
30th May, 1915.

Dear old Girl,

Just a line or so, which I fear will be late, to wish you many happy returns. I suppose I shall have to forget these occasions very shortly, or at least to pretend to. Am enclosing a poundnote for you to get yourself some oddments, as there is nothing to be had out here. I went into Dunkirk for lunch today—everyone was very cheery. I had a wonderful view of part of the front this evening, every trench and shell hole standing out with extraordinary clearness. Am hoping to be home again before long.

Very best love.

Ever your loving brother,
Harold.

30

TO HIS FATHER

No. 1 Wing, R.N.A.S.,
B. Squadron, B.E.F.
1st June, 1915.

Dear Dad,

Have had quite a number of thrills since I wrote last. Yesterday afternoon I reached a height of 10,400 feet on my Avro on a reconnaissance, which is my height record so far—some vol plané descending.

In the evening we had a 'phone message, "Stand by to attack Zeppelin," and on looking out, there it was as large as life a few miles out to sea and very high. We rushed up to the aerodrome and got off by 8.40 p.m. I went straight out to sea after it and got to 6000 feet in 15 minutes, but was never within ten miles of the thing. I wasn't overtaking it at all, but on the contrary it was gaining on me, and after half an hour I lost sight of it.

The sun, of course, was right down by now and I steered home by various lights on shore, for the coast was quite invisible. Had some difficulty in picking out the aerodrome, although huge petrol flares were out, but made quite a good landing. I came in very flat but never saw the ground at all. I touched it when I thought I was still 50 feet up, and also caught the top of the hedge coming into the aerodrome—it was most deceptive. G——, you will remember, was killed at Hendon through not flattening out soon enough.

We next had some dinner, but mine was spoilt through a message from the Commander, which contained instructions for me to drop bombs on an airship shed at Gontrode, near Ghent. The moon rose soon after midnight and at 1.30 a.m. I started off. Things in general have a most depressing aspect at that hour of the morning. I went out to sea via Zeebrugge, and then cut inland.

When I arrived at the place, there was a thick ground mist and dawn was just breaking. I could not see the sheds at all, but two searchlights were going hard. I half circled round, when lo I and behold! I sighted the Zeppelin coming home over Zeebrugge. I turned off due east to avoid being seen, intending to wait until he came down and then to catch him sitting. But my luck was out. One of the searchlights picked me up, and anti-aircraft guns immediately opened fire on me.

Then a curious thing happened. The Zeppelin sighted me (I think the searchlights were signalling) and immediately came for me. This

A Zeppelin airship being used for training personnel at the Johannisthal aerodrome, near Berlin

A Zeppelin in the double shed at Johannisthal, with the smaller Parseval shed next door

A Taube-type German monoplane

was the tables turned on me with a vengeance, and the very last thing I ever dreamt of. It was a regular nightmare. I was only 6000 feet up, and the Zepp, which was very fast, must have been ten. Without being able to get above it, I was, of course, helpless and entirely at the mercy of his maxim guns. I don't think I have been so disconcerted for a long time. We had "some" race! He tried to cut me off from Holland, but I got across his bows.

He was a huge big thing, most imposing, and turned rapidly with the greatest of ease. I hung around north of Ghent, climbing hard, and reached 8,500 feet, but the Zepp wasn't having any. He wasn't coming down while I was there, and I, on the other hand, couldn't get up to him, as he had risen to some fabulous height, so after a bit I pushed off home feeling very discontented at such an unsatisfactory ending. What else could I do? I wasn't going back on the chance of spotting the sheds, with anti-aircraft guns waiting for me below and a Zepp ready to pounce on me from above.

I disposed of my bombs in the sea before landing, and got back after three hours in the air—eventually got to bed at something after 6 a.m. Have been in to see the Commander today, and he was kind enough to tell me I had done all that was possible. He also gave me a little job, which necessitates my getting away soon after midnight tonight. Pray the Lord my engine holds out!

Love to all.

Ever your loving son,
Harold.

P.S.—I hear the Zepp dropped bombs at —— . I must have followed him half-way across.

31

TO HIS MOTHER

No. 1 Wing, R.N.S.,
B Squadron, B.E.F.
2nd June, 1915.

Dear Mum,

Just a line to let you know how I fared last night. I left the aerodrome in the moonlight at one in the morning and I did not at all relish it. I went out to sea past Zeebrugge and cut in over Northern Belgium. Could see the lights of Flushing quite plainly, but it was quite hopeless to find my destination, owing to a thick ground mist, so I returned, dropping my bombs on Blankenberghe on the way. I was only away 1¾ hours, and it was just getting light as I got back. I landed with the help of flares and got to bed by 4 a.m.

Love to all.

Ever your loving son,

Harold.

32

To his Father

No. 1 Wing, R.N.A.S.,
B Squadron, B.E.F.
5th June, 1915.

Dear Dad,

Very little news to tell you, but thought you might like a line or so. I saw in the papers that poor old Barnes[1] has been killed and Travers [H. C. Travers, Flt. Sub-Lieut., R.N.] slightly injured. You remember meeting them both at Hendon. Their names appeared in the casualty lists, so I presume it was not an ordinary smash. Have heard no particulars, but I should fancy they both went up at night after the Zepps, and either had an engine failure or misjudged landing. That's another old Hendonite gone, though he wasn't one of the original ones, and don't think he is in the big photo group.

We lost a seaplane pilot out here the other day. He was brought down off Ostend. Also an awfully nice Belgian I know was taken prisoner two days ago. Have returned my Avro to headquarters and am now flying my B.E. again. I only hold the controls just on getting on and on landing. I don't like them [the B.E. machines] in bad weather. They are too automatic. I have been getting some fine views lately of the lines. It's most interesting up this way.

Babington went home some days ago and Sippe is now in charge here. He has been unwell the last three days, so I am left in command of the station—four officers under me, over 30 men, machines, and seven or eight motors of various descriptions. Have hopes of being given a Nieuport in a day or so. They are fast scouts, supposed to do over 90 miles per hour, and should get a Zepp with one with any luck. Don't know when I am rejoining Babington.

Love to all.

Ever your loving son,

Harold.

---

1. Flight Sub-Lieut. Henry Barnes killed in an accident near London, 4th Oct., 1915.

LIEUT. ROSHER FLYING A BRISTOL "BULLET"

A FIRE CAUSED BY LONG-RANGE BOMBARDMENT
PHOTOGRAPHED FROM AN AEROPLANE

FLIGHT SUB-LIEUT. WARNEFORD, V.C., AND HIS
MORANE "PARASOL"

33

To his Mother

No. 1 Wing, R.N.A.S.,
B Squadron, B.E.F.
5th June, 1915.

Dearest Mum,

I think you cannot have been getting all my letters, as I have never let 10 days go by without a line or so. You are so insistent on numerous letters that you must really excuse the margin or I shall reduce to postcards. Yes, I got the five pounds all right and am urgently wanting the other. You don't seem to fully realise yet that I have left Dunkirk, and that there is not, and never has been, such a thing as a bank within miles of the place. The camera and papers turned up yesterday, for which many thanks. Do send *Flight* and the *Aeroplane*. I have not seen them for weeks. Am just about fed up with this place. We are being turned out and having tents up at the aerodrome.

Big haul last night. Warneford [R. A. J. Warneford, V.C., Flt. Sub-Lieut., R.N.] caught a Zepp at 6,000 feet and did it in, and another was caught in its shed by Wilson and Mills [J. S. Wilson, D.S.C.; F. Mills, D.S.C., both Flight Comdrs., R.N.].

There was also a huge fire at the hospital here last night. All the wounded men were got out, and the sands were strewn with them in beds, etc.

Love to all.

Ever your loving son,
Harold.

34

To his Father

No. 1 Wing, R.N.A.S.,
B Squadron, B.E.F.
8th June, 1915.

Dear Dad,

We are now in tents. Great news about Warneford, isn't it? He certainly deserves the V.C. Am going to fly a Nieuport tomorrow.

12th June, 1915.

Things have been going on much as usual the last few days, but tomorrow I am going down south somewhere (I don't yet know where) to do some spotting for the army. Expect to be away about ten days or perhaps two weeks. Address all letters as usual. It will probably be some time before I receive them. I quite expect I shall run across a number of people I know. It should be an interesting visit, plenty of shell fire though, no doubt.

I flew a Nieuport the other day and hope later to get one of my own. Have not yet heard from Babington. Fear our chances of getting away with him are very slender.

Gramophone going strong.

Love to all.

Ever your loving son,
Harold.

35

To his Mother

No.1 Wing, R.N.A.S.,
B Squadron, B.E.F.
19th June, 1915.

Dearest Mum,

It's ages since I wrote, but it can't be helped, as I have been so awfully busy. For the last week I have been in the neighbourhood of La Bassée, and of course by now you have seen in the papers all about the heavy fighting there. The bombardment was terrific, quite impossible to describe. One day, in the afternoon, I saw it all from above. The small section of trenches they were shelling was simply a mass of smoke and dust, a perfect hell. In the evening of the same day I went out in a car to a point of vantage about three miles behind the line. It was a wonderful sight. Though not near enough to see the infantry advancing, we had, all the same, a fine view. Whenever there was a slight lull in the firing, we heard the maxims and the rifles hard at it.

There is no mistaking the battle line in this part of the world—a long, narrow winding blighted patch of land, extending roughly N. and S. as far as the eye can see. In the middle of it two rows of trenches, in places only 50 yards apart, stand out very conspicuously. These are our first line and that of the Huns. Behind each are the second and third lines, with little zigzag communicating trenches between. It is most interesting. There are some beastly Archies [anti-aircraft guns] though, which come unpleasantly near first shot. Machines are being hit day after day.

Am more or less comfortable on the whole, but running short of socks and hankies. Am also being bitten to death and "hae my doots" about their being mosquitoes. Terrible trouble with machines.

I crashed an undercarriage the other day and cannot get an engine to go. Isn't it terrible news about Warneford? He fell out of his machine, not being strapped in. Babington is in hospital. His foot is giving him trouble again, so fear we shall not get away with him yet awhile.

The dust out here is appalling. Will write again as soon as I can.

Best love to all.

Ever your loving son,
Harold.

36

To his Father

No. 1 Squadron, Royal Flying Corps, B.E.F.
24th June, 1915.

Dear Dad,

Very little news. From what I can see, we are likely to be down here for at least another two weeks. I don't much mind, as in a way I would sooner be here for a little. The change though has rather worn off. Am not a bit comfortable, my billet being a horrible dirty place, with all sorts of weird odours. Food pretty fair, but none too clean, and all eating utensils invariably very dirty.

I suppose tennis is in full swing at home. Pity I'm not due for another spot of leave yet. I got the parcel of papers all right, but not *Flight* and the *Aeroplane*. Think they must have gone astray.

No. 1 Wing, R.N.A.S., B.E.F.
21st July, 1915.

I flew my old B.E. back here [Dunkirk] yesterday, as it has been hot stuffed [requisitioned]. I admit it is rather a dud, but I had no wish to exchange it for a Voisin. After some little trouble I persuaded the Commander to let me have a Morane instead, and tried quite a nice one this morning, the first time I have flown one since I smashed. They are beastly unstable things, and I fully expect to turn this one over before the week is out.

The Commander is keeping me here for a few days' rest before returning to the R.F.C. Dunkirk is quite a lively place nowadays. The Huns have dropped bombs on the aerodrome twice in the last week, but fortunately none of the lads were killed.

Love to all.

Ever your loving son,
Harold.

Note

On the 25th July, 1915, Harold Rosher arrived home on two days' leave, having come across to attend a conference.

37

To his Father

No. 1 Wing, R.N.A.S., B.E.F.
28th July, 1915.

Dear Dad,

Have had a ripping journey back. The country down to Folkestone was just too lovely for words, especially round Ashford. Saw Milverton [the house where he was born] on the way. Had a first-rate crossing, and was met by one of the Rolls [Rolls-Royce car] at Boulogne, so your wire arrived all right. Had lunch at the "Folkestone" before starting back, and then a topping run here. Went out to see the lads at F—— in the evening. Sippe is back again and Baillie in great form. He sends his chin chins, and I gave him yours.

A Hun came over at midnight last night and bombed us. His eight bombs fell nearly a mile away, though.

31st July, 1915.

More excitement. I was due for an anti-aircraft patrol this morning, and just as I was ready, a little before 4.0 a.m,, a Hun machine came over and bombed us. Three bombs fell within a hundred yards of me. I went up after him at once, but lost sight of him in the air, so continued the usual patrol. When I got back, I found that six other machines had followed the first, arriving about fifteen minutes after. None of their bombs did any damage at all. They seem determined to *strafe* this place. A regular cloud of machines goes up after them whenever they appear, but we haven't had much luck as yet.

Expect to be stationed at Dover again in about ten days, for a little while anyhow. The Commander seems to think I don't look fit enough to go out to the Dardanelles. Apparently they are being bowled over with dysentery.

Love to all

Ever your loving son,
Harold.

7

On Home Service Again

38

TO HIS FATHER

R.N. Flying School, Eastchurch.

3rd August, 1915.

Dear Dad,

I left Dover yesterday afternoon on B.E. 2 C, and had a convenient engine failure at Westgate. Landed in the aerodrome and had a chat with Maude before proceeding. Arrived here in due course—it is a most desolate spot. Shall be here anything between three days and three weeks. Saw Babington here soon after I arrived.

10th August, 1915.

I don't seem to be able to get away from this damn war. Last night "old man Zepp" came over here—*"beaucoup de bombs,"*--*"pas de success."* Two machines went up to spikebozzle him, but, of course, never even saw him. A sub went up from Westgate and came down in standing corn. He turned two somersaults.

Have just heard that he has since died. I knew him slightly. We have a terrific big bomb hole in the middle of the aerodrome and numerous smaller ones at the back. Expect to be back in Dunkirk on Sunday next. *"Pas de Dardanelles."* We are going into khaki though.

Love to all.

Ever your loving son,

Harold.

39
TO HIS FATHER

Hotel Burlington, Dover.
12th August, 1915.

Dear Dad,

Have just arrived here from Eastchurch, having been suddenly re-called, and am now told to be ready to cross to Dunkirk in half an hour—no gear, dirty linen, "*pas de leave*"—what a life!

Shall try hard to get some leave in a week or so's time. Anyhow I must get my khaki outfit.

Love.

Your loving son,

Harold.

8

With the B.E.F. Once More

40

TO HIS MOTHER

No. 1 Wing, R.N.A.S., B.E.F.
13th August, 1915.

Dearest Mum,

Got aboard and were off by 8.0 p.m. last night—our ship a comic old tramp with absolutely no accommodation. It took us 6 hours to make Dunkirk and we were not allowed off until 8.0 a.m. this morning. Spent the night walking about or trying to get a little sleep on deck—thank God! it was not rough. We are all "fed to the teeth!" In all probability we shall remain out here another six months now.

The Zepp that was bombed from here had actually been towed right into Ostend harbour. Everyone that went had his machine hit, and one man is missing. This place was bombarded again the other day with the big gun. Expect we are in for a merry time.

Love.

Ever your loving son,
Harold.

41

TO HIS MOTHER

No. 1 Wing, R.N.A.S., B.E.F.
26th August, 1915.

Dearest Mum,

I am being kept very busy out here. Last night there was a comic raid on the Forest of Houthulst. It is six or seven miles behind the lines near Dixmude, and the Huns use it as a rest camp—*beaucoup de* stores and ammunition there too. The French idea was to set it on fire with incendiary bombs. Over forty machines took part, including self—perfect weather conditions—no clouds but very hazy, so when one got high up one was almost invisible. I got just over 11,000 feet, but even then had one or two shots near me. Below me the air was simply a mass of bursting shrapnel. French artillery also opened fire on the place. There must have been *beaucoup de* noise in the forest. Most amusing—a really soft job as someone remarked.

Love to all.

Your loving son,

Harold.

Note

The French official account of the raid described in the foregoing letter was as follows:—

A remarkable series of air raids against German positions or works of military value are reported in yesterday's Paris *communiqués*. In two of them the air squadrons were larger than any previously reported since the beginning of the war.

In one 62 French airmen took part. . . .

The other great raid was undertaken by airmen of the British, French, and Belgian armies, and the British and French navies, to the number of 60. Acting in concert, they attacked the Forest of Houthulst, in Belgium, north-east of Ypres. Several fires broke out. All the aeroplanes returned safely. . . . Previously the largest squadron of attacking aeroplanes was one of 48 machines—of which 40 were British—which attacked the Belgian coast on February 16th last.

42

TO HIS FATHER

No. 1 Wing, R.N.A.S., B.E.F.
26th August, 1915.

Dear Dad,

What do you think of the 40 warships bombarding Zeebrugge? We were all due out there, of course, some spotting, and fighters to protect the spotters. As luck would have it, the weather was dud—clouds at 1,500 feet—with the result that no one got there except a solitary fighter, and he was rewarded by a scrap with a German seaplane. I got just past Ostend, but gave it up as engine was running none too well.

By the way, Bigsworth [A. W. Bigsworth, D.S.O., Squadron Comdr., R.N.] this morning dropped a 60 lb. bomb bang on top of a German submarine and completely did it in—jolly good work.

29th August 1915.

As things stand at present I understand I am not going out to the Dardanelles. I must say I am awfully disappointed, as I was always rather keen to go out there, but I may possibly have a better job. For all I know it may be to rejoin Babington.

Went out to Furnes yesterday afternoon to collect more of my gear. While out there, a German machine came over and dropped six bombs on us. One went right into our tent and three fell within forty yards of me. No one was hit. We all ran like stags.

2nd September, 1915.

Many thanks for your numerous letters, including two forwarded, and *beaucoup de* periodicals. With luck I shall be home in time for your birthday.

Many alterations are taking place here and we are being sadly split up. Andreae and I are very soon going to Dover to join a mythical "C" group. At present Andreae and I are its sole components—even a Squadron Commander is not yet appointed. I am to be 1st Lieut., good for me, but fear they may yet put in a Flight Commander. In all probability we shall be in England over two months. Shall know a heap more in a few days.

9th September, 1915.

Very little news except that we had the monitors bombarding Ostend the day before yesterday. It was a fine sight from the air. A Frenchman was badly hit in the leg going out there, but went on, dropped his bombs and got back. He is not expected to live. Another Frenchman broke his leg this morning in an accident. Four new subs have turned up here and I am to go home as soon as they can fly the fast machines—it should be within ten days. I ought to have gone home by rights about two weeks ago. Am flying over when I eventually do come. The last two machines that went over both crashed at Folkestone—shall probably do the same.

Love to all.

Ever your loving son,
Harold.

9

On Home Service Once More

43

To his Father

Hotel Burlington, Dover
13th September, 1915.

Dear Dad,

Am back again in England at last and am expecting to get two weeks' leave in a day or so. I got here at midday yesterday, having flown over from Dunkirk on a Nieuport. Drove out to Margate yesterday afternoon with Spenser Grey. Shall probably go out again on the 1st December.

14th September, 1915.

Just a line to let you know my probable movements. Though I am due for two weeks' leave, it seems improbable that I shall get it just yet awhile, but shall not be returning to Dunkirk until December 1st, when I shall remain out there for two months.

I have just taken over the 1st Lieutenant's job on this station, and this is keeping me busy no end. I am the senior officer, bar the C.O., in fact 2nd in Command, and am responsible for everything going on at the station, *i.e.* all executive work, etc. It is, of course, all new to me, and I find myself at sea every now and again. It is, however, a great opportunity. You should see me take parades (divisions, we call them), swish!

Please send me on, as soon as possible, my new monkey jacket and new pair of trousers, also new hat My present uniform is most disreputable, covered in oil, etc., and must be scrapped at the earliest opportunity.

A Bristol Scout biplane or "bullet"

The Morane "parasol" monoplane
Flown by Flight Sub-Lieut. Warneford, V. C., when he
destroyed a Zeppelin

29th September, 1915.

I knew I should forget it, your birthday I mean. I suddenly remembered it whilst shaving this morning. I have been carrying a two-year-old notebook about with me too, to remind me, as it was marked in it—*pas de* good though, and it's such a long time ago now. *Beaucoup de* work, or I would have written sooner.

I have just heard a nasty rumour that I am returning to Dunkirk on October 15th. We are getting 40 subs down here in a few days. That means tons more work for me.

4th October, 1915.

I think I shall get my leave (10 days only) next week. Risk [Major C. E. Risk, Squadron Commander, R.N.] asked me if I would like to remain here as 1st Lieutenant, an awful question to decide. I think I shall let things stay as they are and take my flight out to Dunkirk on October 15th. It seems too much like giving in to stay here.

30th October, 1915.

You picked me out a ripping train! It took me four hours to get down here with a change at Faversham. When I arrived at the Priory Station I was told it would be half an hour before the train could proceed to the Harbour, so had to get out and walk. I got in here at ten past ten, and the last straw was that Betty had no sandwiches left.

Graham [C. W. Graham, D.S.O., Flt. Lieut., R.N.] nearly killed himself this afternoon. He got into a spinning nose dive on a Morane parasol, and by the Grace of God got out again at 500 feet. In all probability I shall get my leave after this next lot of pilots have gone out to Dunkirk, but that remains to be seen.

14th November, 1915.

Am postponing my leave until still later, as it is rather important for me to stay here at the moment. Good things so very rarely come off though. I shall be most bitterly disappointed, however, if another two months does not see me on Active Service again.

30th November, 1915.

Can you come down this weekend? I have great hopes that Husky and Baillie will be back from the other side.

Apparently they had quite a good bag a day or so ago, one Hun seaplane, one submarine, and a bomb bang in the middle of a T.B.D. [torpedo boat destroyer].

Risk is away most of this week, but should be back by Saturday. He flew a Maurice over from Dunkirk last week and made quite a landing on arrival.

15th December, 1915.

I so much enjoyed my too short weekend. I fear I shall not be able to get up to town again until after Xmas. Had quite a nice journey down, making Stewart's [W. S. Stewart, Flt. Sub-Lieut., R.N.] acquaintance on the way, likewise his wife's.

Risk said he thought I had been away months and seemed quite relieved to see me back again. Graham and Ince [S. Ince, D.S.C., Flt. Sub-Lieut, R.N.] have put up a first-rate performance. They were not shot down. Graham came down low to see the Huns in the water, and his engine never picked up again. The Hun machine caught fire, and must have had bombs on it, for it exploded on hitting the water. Both machines fell bang in the middle of the fleet, which was duly impressed. Graham, of course, turned a somersault, and both he and Ince were nearly drowned.

1st January, 1916.

Had a great evening last night. A crowd of us went to dinner with G—— to see the New Year in. We did it in style. Tomorrow I am lunching with the Bax-Ironsides.[1]

I looped on a B.E. 2 C. in great form the other day. If I had not been very securely strapped in, I should have fallen clean out. As it was, the cushion in the passenger's seat fell out and vanished. One seems to be upside down for a frightfully long time.

I did the trick out in the country at between three and four thousand feet. The first time I had barely enough speed, so had a second shot and got up to over 100 knots. I really thought the wings would fall off. We had two topping crashes yesterday, but neither of the pilots hurt.

Tons of love and a prosperous New Year.

Ever your loving son,
Harold.

44

To his Grandmother

Hotel Burlington, Dover.
27th September, 1915.

Dear Granny,

Am so sorry to hear you have been having such a rotten time, but

---

1. Sir Henry Bax-Ironside, late Minister in Bulgaria.

trust you are by now well on the road to recovery.

I have been having an awfully busy time lately. The King came down here to inspect us on Thursday, and shook hands with all the officers in the afternoon.

Am by degrees helping to get together another squadron to go out to Dunkirk. We are due across there half way through next ' month. I am not particularly anxious to go out again just yet, unless we can really get a move on.

I hope before I go to get a little leave. I am due for two weeks, so may see you in the near future.

Heaps of love.

Your loving grandson,
Harold.

45

To his Father

Hotel Burlington, Dover.
3rd January, 1916.

Dear Dad,

I have got wind of something rather priceless . . . for when the war is over, I will tell you a little about this scheme, only remember it's strictly private and confidential, so you must not mention it to anyone.

In a nutshell it's this, a flight from —— to ——. It sounds rather impossible at first, but I think quite a number of people would have a shot if they could get someone to pay expenses. This is where I get a look in.

The experience anyhow would be wonderful. One of the subs here has just put me up to it, and says he has everything arranged. That sounds rather rapid, but he has written for an appointment, so I shall be able to let you know later how things go. In the meanwhile lie doggo and do come down this weekend, if possible, so that we can talk things over.

Very best love.

Ever your loving son,
Harold.

46

To his Mother

Hotel Burlington, Dover.
4th February, 1915.

Dearest Mum,

Just a short line to let you know I am crossing to Dunkirk tomorrow, weather permitting. I am flying a R.A.F. B.E. across and returning the same day, in a Nieuport if available, otherwise in a destroyer. Am quite looking forward to the trip. Have already crossed the Channel three times by air and about twelve by water.

Beaucoup de love.

Your loving son,
Harold.

47

To his Father

Hotel Burlington, Dover.
5th February, 1916.

Dear Dad,

Had a most interesting day yesterday. Started off across Channel for Dunkirk soon after 8.0 a.m. in a R.A.F. B.E.—engine running badly at first, but picked up. A most priceless morning with a slight following wind—5,000 feet at Calais, and made Dunkirk in about ¾ hour from here.

All the lads in great form, but Petre [J. J. Petre, D.S.C., Flt. Comdr., R.N.] and Peberdy [W. H. Peberdy, F. Sub-Lieut., R.N.] in Paris, and Mulock [R. H. Mulock, D.S.O., Flt. Comdr., R.N.] in hospital with a chill.

Baillie going strong, also Beard [G. H. Beard, D.S.C., Flt. Comdr., R.N.], Haskins [F. K. Haskins, D.S.C., Squadron Comdr., R.N.], Graham, Peal [Lieut. E. R. Peal, D.S.C., R.N.V.R.], *etc., etc.* Breakfast and then a good look round. The Baby Nieuports are priceless. I flew one and went up the coast to La Panne and Fumes. When I got back I drove out to Caudekirk to the new aerodrome, and then back for lunch.

At 2.0 p.m. I started home in a Nieuport and made Folkestone in just over the hour—rather a strong head wind. At Folkestone I spent 1½ hours trying to restart my engine, but with no success, so telephoned for a car—tea at the Grand and back here in time for dinner. Have been to Folkestone this afternoon with Ince and his brother

A B.E. 2C BIPLANE

A NIEUPORT BIPLANE
COMMONLY KNOWN AS A "1½ PLANE" OWING TO THE SMALLER
LOWER PLANE

A BLÉRIOT MONOPLANE

and Husky.

Heaps of love.

Ever your loving son,
Harold.

P.S.—Flew back at 2,000 feet.

48

TO HIS MOTHER

Hotel Burlington, Dover.
9th February, 1916.

Dearest Mum,

Many thanks for letter. Am still going strong. Flew four different types of machines today, two of them new ones, one a Shorthorn Maurice, and the other a Blériot. The Blériot is the first monoplane I have flown other than a parasol.

You have heard me mention Graham (with Ince he brought down the German seaplane). Well, he has just had an awful bad crash at Dunkirk.

Penley [C. F. B. Penley, Flt. Sub-Lieut, R.N.] also has crashed badly twice out there, and is now back on sick leave. Ford [E. L. Ford, Flt. Sub-Lieut., R.N.] too is home on sick leave with his head cut open, as the result of a bad crash, and his passenger is not expected to live. If one goes on flying long enough, one is bound to get huffed [killed] in the end.

By the way, Commander Lambe [Capt. C. L. Lambe, Wing Captain, R.N.] has shipped another stripe. He is now Wing Captain and acting Captain.

Yesterday I flew to Chingford in a B.E. 2 C. with Blanch [N. C. Blanch, Flt. Sub-Lieut, R.N.] as passenger. It was awfully cold. It took 2½ hours going, via Ashford, Redhill, Brooklands and Hendon. Blanch took the B.E. back, and I took a new Bristol Scout and did the return journey direct (east of London) in an hour. Saw the Pemberton-Billing quadruplane at Chingford.

Best love.

Ever your loving son,
Harold.

49

To his Father

Hotel Burlington, Dover,
11th February, 1916.

Dear Dad,

Had hopes of seeing you for a few minutes today. Had the weather been fine, Husky and I were motoring to town in the morning with Capt. Lambe in a Rolls, and both bringing machines back in the afternoon from Chingford. As it is, of course, the weather is impossible.

I was away first, in under three minutes, the other day when the Germans were reported over Ramsgate. I was over the North Foreland in quarter of an hour at 6,000 feet. Was just turning, when I sighted a seaplane miles below me, so cut off my petrol, and did a spiral vol plané towards it.

At 4,000 feet I ran into mist and lost him temporarily, but picked him up again and chased him up the mouth of the Thames almost as far as Herne Bay. Then he turned and shot under me, and I'm blessed if it wasn't a Schneider Cup, one of our own machines from Westgate! I did not hear that bombs had been dropped until I saw it in the papers the following morning. I thought the scare was about our own seaplane.

Visited the Blimps [small airships] this afternoon at Capel. They are really most interesting.

13th February, 1916.

Many thanks for note received this morning. As far as I can see, there is no chance of my going out to the other side yet awhile. Husky goes on the 25th and Andreae a little later. Two good crashes today. First Blanch on a new Avro—engine failure and landed downwind in a ploughed field. The second was better still. A man hit the one and only tree within miles, in getting off on a B.E. He left half a lower plane in the tree and carried a branch or so on with him for some little distance before crashing to earth.

I hear Graham is no better. He fractured the base of his skull and also has internal injuries.

Love to all.

Ever your loving son,
Harold.

50

To his Mother

Hotel Burlington, Dover.
20th February, 1916.

Dearest Mum,

Another raid on Deal today, five bombs dropped and one man killed. I took over the War flight this morning, and had a patrol in the air at the time. I myself and others were off within a few minutes of receiving the signal, but no one even saw the machine.

Over sixty ratings arrived this morning without warning, and I had to make all arrangements for them to be fed, housed and washed. All of them were Derby recruits and had been in the Service 24 hours, mostly graded as A.M. 2nd class. None had seen an aeroplane before. They were butchers, grocers, cotton spinners, weavers, etc.

The C.O. goes away tomorrow for two weeks. Sippe, Andreae, Husky, Viney [T. E. Viney, D.S.O., Flt. Lieut. R.N.], etc. go to Paris in a day or so, and I am left to run the Station, School and War flight, keeping up a continuous patrol with four machines.

Love to all.

Your loving son,
Harold.

51

To his Father

Hotel Burlington, Dover.
24th February, 1916.

Dear Dad,

Many thanks for letter received yesterday.

Risk is still in town. I would far sooner get out East somewhere than any home station or Dunkirk. I understand shortly there will be great alterations in the R.N.A.S. Rumour has it again that we are to give up land machines entirely and stick to seaplanes.

Drove over to Eastchurch yesterday on business, roads in places 18" deep in snow. Coming back I had a priceless skid and finished up in a ditch. No one hurt or even shaken. Returned here by train, and car came on today. It was very little damaged, steering arm bent, and one wheel slightly out of truth. It was really rather comic.

Did you hear how Usborne and Ireland [3] were killed? If not, will

3. Wing-Commander Neville F. Usborne, R.N., and Squadron Commander de C. W. P. Ireland, R.N. were killed 23rd Feb., 1916.

tell you later. T—— was burnt to death.
     Love to all.

                 Ever your loving son,
                       Harold.

LEONAUR

ALSO FROM LEONAUR
AVAILABLE IN SOFTCOVER OR HARDCOVER WITH DUST JACKET

THE FALL OF THE MOGHUL EMPIRE OF HINDUSTAN *by H. G. Keene*—By the beginning of the nineteenth century, as British and Indian armies under Lake and Wellesley dominated the scene, a little over half a century of conflict brought the Moghul Empire to its knees.

LADY SALE'S AFGHANISTAN *by Florentia Sale*—An Indomitable Victorian Lady's Account of the Retreat from Kabul During the First Afghan War.

THE CAMPAIGN OF MAGENTA AND SOLFERINO 1859 *by Harold Carmichael Wylly*—The Decisive Conflict for the Unification of Italy.

FRENCH'S CAVALRY CAMPAIGN *by J. G. Maydon*—A Special Corresponent's View of British Army Mounted Troops During the Boer War.

CAVALRY AT WATERLOO *by Sir Evelyn Wood*—British Mounted Troops During the Campaign of 1815.

THE SUBALTERN *by George Robert Gleig*—The Experiences of an Officer of the 85th Light Infantry During the Peninsular War.

NAPOLEON AT BAY, 1814 *by F. Loraine Petre*—The Campaigns to the Fall of the First Empire.

NAPOLEON AND THE CAMPAIGN OF 1806 *by Colonel Vachée*—The Napoleonic Method of Organisation and Command to the Battles of Jena & Auerstädt.

THE COMPLETE ADVENTURES IN THE CONNAUGHT RANGERS *by William Grattan*—The 88th Regiment during the Napoleonic Wars by a Serving Officer.

BUGLER AND OFFICER OF THE RIFLES *by William Green & Harry Smith*—With the 95th (Rifles) during the Peninsular & Waterloo Campaigns of the Napoleonic Wars.

NAPOLEONIC WAR STORIES *by Sir Arthur Quiller-Couch*—Tales of soldiers, spies, battles & sieges from the Peninsular & Waterloo campaigns.

CAPTAIN OF THE 95TH (RIFLES) *by Jonathan Leach*—An officer of Wellington's sharpshooters during the Peninsular, South of France and Waterloo campaigns of the Napoleonic wars.

RIFLEMAN COSTELLO *by Edward Costello*—The adventures of a soldier of the 95th (Rifles) in the Peninsular & Waterloo Campaigns of the Napoleonic wars.

LEONAUR

ALSO FROM LEONAUR
AVAILABLE IN SOFTCOVER OR HARDCOVER WITH DUST JACKET

AT THEM WITH THE BAYONET by Donald F. Featherstone—The first Anglo-Sikh War 1845-1846.

STEPHEN CRANE'S BATTLES by Stephen Crane—Nine Decisive Battles Recounted by the Author of 'The Red Badge of Courage'.

THE GURKHA WAR by H. T. Prinsep—The Anglo-Nepalese Conflict in North East India 1814-1816.

FIRE & BLOOD by G. R. Gleig—The burning of Washington & the battle of New Orleans, 1814, through the eyes of a young British soldier.

SOUND ADVANCE! by Joseph Anderson—Experiences of an officer of HM 50th regiment in Australia, Burma & the Gwalior war.

THE CAMPAIGN OF THE INDUS by Thomas Holdsworth—Experiences of a British Officer of the 2nd (Queen's Royal) Regiment in the Campaign to Place Shah Shuja on the Throne of Afghanistan 1838 - 1840.

WITH THE MADRAS EUROPEAN REGIMENT IN BURMA by John Butler—The Experiences of an Officer of the Honourable East India Company's Army During the First Anglo-Burmese War 1824 - 1826.

IN ZULULAND WITH THE BRITISH ARMY by Charles L. Norris-Newman—The Anglo-Zulu war of 1879 through the first-hand experiences of a special correspondent.

BESIEGED IN LUCKNOW by Martin Richard Gubbins—The first Anglo-Sikh War 1845-1846.

A TIGER ON HORSEBACK by L. March Phillips—The Experiences of a Trooper & Officer of Rimington's Guides - The Tigers - during the Anglo-Boer war 1899 - 1902.

SEPOYS, SIEGE & STORM by Charles John Griffiths—The Experiences of a young officer of H.M.'s 61st Regiment at Ferozepore, Delhi ridge and at the fall of Delhi during the Indian mutiny 1857.

CAMPAIGNING IN ZULULAND by W. E. Montague—Experiences on campaign during the Zulu war of 1879 with the 94th Regiment.

THE STORY OF THE GUIDES by G.J. Younghusband—The Exploits of the Soldiers of the famous Indian Army Regiment from the northwest frontier 1847 - 1900.

LEONAUR

ALSO FROM LEONAUR

AVAILABLE IN SOFTCOVER OR HARDCOVER WITH DUST JACKET

THE RELUCTANT REBEL by William G. Stevenson—A young Kentuckian's experiences in the Confederate Infantry & Cavalry during the American Civil War..

BOOTS AND SADDLES by Elizabeth B. Custer—The experiences of General Custer's Wife on the Western Plains.

FANNIE BEERS' CIVIL WAR by Fannie A. Beers—A Confederate Lady's Experiences of Nursing During the Campaigns & Battles of the American Civil War.

LADY SALE'S AFGHANISTAN by Florentia Sale—An Indomitable Victorian Lady's Account of the Retreat from Kabul During the First Afghan War.

THE TWO WARS OF MRS DUBERLY by Frances Isabella Duberly—An Intrepid Victorian Lady's Experience of the Crimea and Indian Mutiny.

THE REBELLIOUS DUCHESS by Paul F. S. Dermoncourt—The Adventures of the Duchess of Berri and Her Attempt to Overthrow French Monarchy.

LADIES OF WATERLOO by Charlotte A. Eaton, Magdalene de Lancey & Juana Smith—The Experiences of Three Women During the Campaign of 1815: Waterloo Days by Charlotte A. Eaton, A Week at Waterloo by Magdalene de Lancey & Juana's Story by Juana Smith.

TWO YEARS BEFORE THE MAST by Richard Henry Dana. Jr.—The account of one young man's experiences serving on board a sailing brig—the Penelope—bound for California, between the years1834-36.

A SAILOR OF KING GEORGE by Frederick Hoffman—From Midshipman to Captain—Recollections of War at Sea in the Napoleonic Age 1793-1815.

LORDS OF THE SEA by A. T. Mahan—Great Captains of the Royal Navy During the Age of Sail.

COGGESHALL'S VOYAGES: VOLUME 1 by George Coggeshall—The Recollections of an American Schooner Captain.

COGGESHALL'S VOYAGES: VOLUME 2 by George Coggeshall—The Recollections of an American Schooner Captain.

TWILIGHT OF EMPIRE by Sir Thomas Ussher & Sir George Cockburn—Two accounts of Napoleon's Journeys in Exile to Elba and St. Helena: Narrative of Events by Sir Thomas Ussher & Napoleon's Last Voyage: Extract of a diary by Sir George Cockburn.

LEONAUR

ALSO FROM LEONAUR

AVAILABLE IN SOFTCOVER OR HARDCOVER WITH DUST JACKET

FARAWAY CAMPAIGN *by F. James*—Experiences of an Indian Army Cavalry Officer in Persia & Russia During the Great War.

REVOLT IN THE DESERT *by T. E. Lawrence*—An account of the experiences of one remarkable British officer's war from his own perspective.

MACHINE-GUN SQUADRON *by A. M. G.*—The 20th Machine Gunners from British Yeomanry Regiments in the Middle East Campaign of the First World War.

A GUNNER'S CRUSADE *by Antony Bluett*—The Campaign in the Desert, Palestine & Syria as Experienced by the Honourable Artillery Company During the Great War .

DESPATCH RIDER *by W. H. L. Watson*—The Experiences of a British Army Motorcycle Despatch Rider During the Opening Battles of the Great War in Europe.

TIGERS ALONG THE TIGRIS *by E. J. Thompson*—The Leicestershire Regiment in Mesopotamia During the First World War.

HEARTS & DRAGONS *by Charles R. M. F. Crutwell*—The 4th Royal Berkshire Regiment in France and Italy During the Great War, 1914-1918.

INFANTRY BRIGADE: 1914 *by John Ward*—The Diary of a Commander of the 15th Infantry Brigade, 5th Division, British Army, During the Retreat from Mons.

DOING OUR 'BIT' *by Ian Hay*—Two Classic Accounts of the Men of Kitchener's 'New Army' During the Great War including *The First 100,000* & *All In It*.

AN EYE IN THE STORM *by Arthur Ruhl*—An American War Correspondent's Experiences of the First World War from the Western Front to Gallipoli-and Beyond.

STAND & FALL *by Joe Cassells*—With the Middlesex Regiment Against the Bolsheviks 1918-19.

RIFLEMAN MACGILL'S WAR *by Patrick MacGill*—A Soldier of the London Irish During the Great War in Europe including *The Amateur Army*, *The Red Horizon* & *The Great Push*.

WITH THE GUNS *by C. A. Rose & Hugh Dalton*—Two First Hand Accounts of British Gunners at War in Europe During World War 1- Three Years in France with the Guns and With the British Guns in Italy.

THE BUSH WAR DOCTOR *by Robert V. Dolbey*—The Experiences of a British Army Doctor During the East African Campaign of the First World War.